MW00444721

Another Day

ANOTHER DAY IN THE LIFE OF A COUNTRY VET

FRED NEWSCHWANDER DVM

DECEMBER 2018

Another Day

CONTENTS

INTRODUCTION

A year has passed since January 2018 when I published "A Day in the Life of a Country Vet". Subsequently, other stories that accumulated and were buried in the dusty memory catacombs of my brain have been attempting escape.

From time to time I consider my good fortune and remind myself that: ***Today I Set a Personal Best Record for the Most Consecutive Days Lived***. The thickening hair coats of my dog Piper, my cat DC (Doc's Cat), and my horses Slider and Morticia indicated that winter was upon us and it had gotten too cold to saddle up and ride. Therefore, I resolved to settle in at my keyboard near the fireplace to document and pass on more stories of the animals, people, and places that so enriched my years as a mixed animal veterinarian. Here is **"Another Day in the Life of a Country Vet."**. Hopefully my effort will entertain and fill your evening leisure hours.

Another Day

STRONG WIND WARNING

They say the wind can blow pretty hard in these here parts. The evidence is not hard to find. It kind of socks you right in the kisser or even knocks you down. The trees all tilt to the southeast because the wind blows from the northwest. We always seem to have a Nor'wester brewing. Someone once attempted to establish a Christmas tree farm but there seemed to be a limited market for firs or pines that were all bent in one direction and had virtually no branches on the windward side. They were perfect if you had a leaning crooked house or wanted to put the Christmas tree up against the wall or in a corner to hide the naked side. I think this tree business must be why the earth spins around towards the east; in the direction the wind blows. The trees act like green sails and drag the earth around with them. I used to have hair but the wind appears to have ripped most of it out, because now I'm bald on top. Dang that wind!

There seems to be a shortage of dirt in the northwestern part of the county; just a few inches of coarse gritty soil between the sage and rabbit brush on top of 17-million-year-old dark basalt rocks. Digging a fence post hole can be an all-day job because there is inevitably a bowling ball sized rock right in the bottom of the hole (but you could get lucky and find an Ellensburg blue agate instead). If you travel downwind to the southeast part of the county, an area called Badger Pocket, the topsoil is very fine fertile wind deposited loess. Guess where all that nice dirt came from; the upwind end of the county. Sports events can be very interesting. Once in a high school football game I kicked off into the wind of a snow storm. It was blowing so hard it blew the ball right back to me and I caught my own kickoff. Track meet sprint records are meaningless if there is a 25mph tailwind. It has been said that when children get off the school bus, the parents might need to go to the downwind neighbor's house to pick them up. A gust of wind could just tumble them on down the road like weeds with sneakers and a backpack. If the parents weren't home the bus just dropped the kids off at the next stop upwind from their home to be eventually deposited at the proper driveway. Similarly, you might find your newspaper in the downwind neighbor's box. It's not uncommon to see bales of hay lying alongside the freeway or even overturned truckloads. It's only our normal springtime zephyrs doing their usual stuff.

There is a geological/meteorological explanation for our wind. Snoqualmie Pass, and the Columbia River Gorge, are the lowest points in the Cascade Mountain Range. When weather fronts come in from the Pacific Ocean, they travel more easily through these lower areas. This funnels the wind up the Columbia River Gorge or right down our Yakima River valley. In the spring of each year, the wind can blow nonstop for days on end. One spring I had to ride my bicycle to school (uphill and against the wind both coming and going, barefoot, temperature well below zero, and snowing.) and marked off 42 successive windy calendar days.

One of the more dramatic examples of the power of the wind is sometimes observed by people traveling through the valley. Spring is calving time and the cows are out in calving paddocks delivering their babies which are quickly followed by the afterbirth. It is said that the wind can blow so hard that it will lift the placenta right up off the ground and deposit it up on power lines, the cross arms on the telephone poles, or branches of trees. There are those doubters that argue, however, that there might be another strange but possible natural explanation for this phenomenon.

Glacier Lake is a beautiful body of water spanning the US border into Canada in the Rocky Mountains of Glacier National Park. The lake is the home of kokanee which are otherwise known as landlocked sockeye salmon. They spawn in the spring in late March or April and eagles from all over the region would gather in that area to feed on the spawning fish. The Fish and Wildlife Department decided that the fishery could be enhanced if there was more food available for the fish. They chose to add a new strain of freshwater shrimp to Glacier Lake hoping to provide more and better food. In retrospect, the new shrimp competed *against* the fish and in fact were eating the native freshwater shrimp that were otherwise food for the fish. The result was the collapse of the fishery and thus a food source during an important stressful time of year for our American icon: The Bald Eagle.

I don't believe that this theory has been scientifically documented but the timing and circumstances are just too strong a coincidence not to have some basis in fact. When the fishery collapsed, the eagles had to find another source of food. It turns out this coincided with calving season in the Kittitas Valley and

11

in the early 1980s there could be four to five hundred bald eagles perching in the trees around calving pastures. The head eagle must have sent out text messages or tweets to all the other eagles alerting them to the newly opened tony restaurant in Kittitas County. Some ranchers feared the birds might be a threat to the calves but this did not prove to be the case. Eagles were here to feed on the delicious nutritious placentas left after calving. Not wanting to share their booty, eagles would pick up these rather heavy bovine pizzas and fly up into a more secluded private dining area. So, in fact, it was not the strong wind but the instinct of a Bald Eagle to secure its food away from other competing eagles that resulted in placentas hanging like obscene Christmas tree ornaments from trees and telephone poles and powerlines.

The springtime eagle numbers are greatly reduced now to 30 or 40. Our cattle numbers have not been this low since the 1800's so one food source has essentially dried up (and blown away). I wonder where they go now? I hear there are some really great new Italian restaurants in the Puget Sound area. I don't know if they serve lasagna a la placenta.

TWO MEN WALKED INTO A BAR

A farmer and a doctor happened, by chance, to meet in a bar during happy hour on a pleasant Friday spring afternoon. They were acquaintances but not good friends. After some clearing of throats and hemming and hawing, the farmer, not wanting to be overheard by the other patrons, said quietly to the doctor, "The strangest thing happened the other day. My English Pointer, Bosco, had been missing for a few days. We usually let him run loose and he sometimes disappears for a day or two so we weren't particularly worried. When he finally showed up at the house, he seemed rather lethargic for a day or two and then gradually regained his usual vigor. He does seem less inclined to wander the neighborhood now and does a better job of staying home. Bosco likes to sleep on his back by the fireplace and I happened to notice yesterday that he had four very neat little

13

stitches between his hind legs. It looked like he could have had some minor surgical procedure but I couldn't really tell for sure. Do you have any idea what could have happened to him?"

The doctor said, "I really have no *idea*, but you might want to take him to your veterinarian and have those stitches removed. I keep my Brittany Spaniel bitches confined in a large heated kennel with an outdoor run. I have noticed that when Sassy is in heat, male dogs, who are not confined, often hang around. Some try and climb over the fence or even dig under it. I don't want any mongrel puppies. I suppose it's *possible* there is some connection."

And now *for the rest of the story* as the famous radio announcer Paul Harvey used to say.

The farmer was actually more of a wealthy agribusiness man and never *lived on the farm*. His family had properties and businesses scattered throughout the region. Money came from alfalfa, grain, potatoes, and wine. He lived on a spacious semi-rural property on the outskirts of town. He like to bird hunt in the fall and usually had several professionally trained and well-bred English Pointers kept for that purpose. He didn't, however, like to keep his boys confined. They had a doggie door that let them in and out of the garage whenever they desired. The net result was that they were free to roam the neighborhood near the city limits and could socialize with other dogs and additionally harass game birds out of season.

The doctor, on the other hand, lived not far away in a rural housing development and also had hunting dogs. He kept his Brittany Spaniels confined and had built them a heated kennel with a nicely fenced large outdoor run. When one of his girls was in heat, the doctor had tried to be patient with the male dogs lurking about, but over time, patience can run thin. He had chased the males away and even sent them home with notes attached to their collars requesting that the dogs not be allowed to roam. But the results had been notably disappointing. He had talked to the sheriff who more or less evaded the problem saying that, "I really don't have the manpower for dog catcher duties." The problem

14

occurred in the county outside of the city limits and animal control regulations, other than livestock protection, were pretty much non-existent. If dogs were harming livestock you did have the legal right to shoot them but this was obviously not what the doctor wanted to do. Rumor has it that the doctor talked to a friend, who just happened to be a veterinarian, for some medical/surgical advice. This was a time before specialization and most MDs also did a fair amount of general surgery. A little bit of hamburger, a little bit of tranquilizer, a little bit of anesthetic, a little bit of neutering surgery, and a little bit of stitching and the problem was solved. Everybody seemed to know what had happened and who were the likely suspects, but nothing could really be proven. We didn't have any VCSI (Veterinary Crime Scene Investigators) eagerly awaiting the opportunity to solve this animal medical mystery.

When you are a prominent wealthy member of the community, it's not difficult to get the ear of other potentially helpful people. Thus, the chief of police, the county sheriff, and several local lawyers became very well acquainted with the story as well. Ultimately, nothing could be proven except in the barber shops, taverns, coffee shops, and card rooms of town. Rumor has it that a nice heated kennel with a large outdoor run was soon constructed on a spacious semi-rural property on the outskirts of town. There was a significant decrease in *dog at large* complaints and a total absence of English Pointer cross bred puppies looking for good homes the following spring.

COWBOYS V VET

The brothers were local hard-working cowboys. They had small ranches of their own they had inherited from their father's hardscrabble split estate but to make financial ends meet and try and get ahead, they helped other cattlemen around the valley by playing *cowboy for hire*. Once they got out of their hard-used Ford 250 pickup trucks, jammed on their battered sweat stained hats, pulled on their manure stained chaps, and strapped on their jingly spurs, they were ready to work. They'd have left the spurs on full time except they sometimes got hung up on the truck floor mats and made driving a bit too adventuresome, or because they ripped the bedsheets. They helped out in the sales barn on Fridays and there weren't too many cowboy or ranch jobs that they hadn't done at some point in time. They also broke and trained horses in what little spare time they had left. That's how I happened to encounter them on that brisk windy late afternoon spring day.

I had just finished up a farm call putting stitches in a horse that got tangled up in barbed wire. (Horses and barbed wire don't mix. The coiled wire just jumps out and strikes the defenseless horse.) When I drifted through a stop sign before pulling out onto the main county highway, I saw the boys trying to load a wild and frightened looking colt into a stock trailer. They had backed the trailer up to a gate in the corral and fashioned a loading chute out of old wooden fence panels. The halter cast aside in the dirt seem to indicate that they had given up trying to catch the horse in the conventional fashion, and they were now mounted on their stock horses with their lariats in hand. It didn't take long to get two ropes on the colt and stretch him out between the two horses. And what to do now? Eventually they fed one of the ropes up the trailer ramp and through the front end of the trailer. The obvious plan was to pull on that rope thus dragging the colt into the trailer. However, the colt wasn't a quitter and it charged into the trailer thinking there might somehow be an escape route. Once inside it continued struggling making the stock trailer jump up and down like an out-of-balance Maytag washing machine. As I sat there watching mesmerized, it continued struggling and rearing up, poked a foot out through one of the openings in the stock trailer walls. Then it fell down and was left hanging there like a rag doll suspended by the trapped leg. I couldn't just sit there watching a horse wind up with a broken leg so I pulled up to the gate to see if I could help. Every time the boys got close enough to see if they could untangle the colt, it commenced thrashing with its three free legs making it impossible to approach. They were in a juggernaut. I suggested that if I knocked the colt out with drugs, we could then safely free the trapped leg. They grudgingly nodded their heads an agreement and said, "Okay have at it." They diplomatically didn't add, "Wise guy."

There was a panel inside the trailer that could offer me some slight protection, so I loaded a syringe with a short-acting anesthetic and ducked inside. I got lucky and when the colt paused for a moment in its struggles. I got a syringe full of drug into his jugular vein and in no time at all, he relaxed and hung there like a side of beef. We quickly jumped inside and the three of us were just able to lift his front end up enough to free the leg. Amazingly there seemed to be no significant injury other than a scrape and a considerable loss of hair on his lower leg. We got the halter on his head and quickly exited the trailer before he could wake up and finish us off.

We climbed up on the fence rails to sit and rest and reflect upon what happened. I certainly had not intended to show the cowboys up or tell them what to do, but obviously they felt a little peeved that my help had been required to extricate them from their predicament. They offered me a warm dusty Budweiser from the floorboards of their truck and one of them said with a smile on his face, "We had things pretty much under control until you showed up." The dented walls and bent side panels on the rugged stock trailer seem to indicate that there was more to the story.

They told me that one of their neighbors had asked them if they would break his colt. They agreed. Eventually the neighbor called back to say that he had been trying just to catch and halter the colt unsuccessfully for a month. That's when he asked them to catch it and take it home to their corrals where they could work with it. That's when we had our little private rodeo.

They put in 30 days and had him working pretty well. However, the neighbor decided that the colt was going to be too much for him and realized he didn't really want to keep it. Horse prices were pretty low at that time so they resolved the financial issue by swapping the training time for the horse. The cowboys eventually put in some pretty serious training and I'm pretty sure I saw one of the boys riding the colt for one of the county roping competitions. He had matured into a well-built bay gelding who seemed to really love working cattle and calf roping competitions. He must have decided he would prefer go to the NFR finals as a tie down roping horse rather than a rough stock bucking horse.

SKUNKED

Was this where it all began? My career working with animals? I grew up on a small rural acreage that our family had acquired so my mother would have a place to keep her horses. Dad never rode but Mother allowed him to feed the horses and shovel manure until I was old enough to earn the privilege. We put up our own hay with the help of a neighbor who had the equipment to cut, rake, and bale the hay. Bob was 11 years older than I, but somehow, we were friends and he put up with the endless questions of his 10-year-old neighbor.

One day he called to say that a mama skunk had been killed by the sickle mowing machine and there was an orphaned baby. Did I want a pet skunk? This was before the rules about owning a wild animal were well established and we were relatively uninformed about the concerns of diseases like rabies. So, I jumped at the opportunity. I grabbed a gunny sack, mounted my trusty Schwinn bicycle, and pedaled furiously the two miles up the road to where Bob lived with his parents. By the time I got there I was pretty overheated so I took off my shirt to cool down. We jumped in his old Chevy flatbed pickup and drove out into the hay field to scope out the scene of the crime. The half-grown baby skunk was a little disoriented, but it was still there on the grassy ditch bank of the irrigation canal. Without really stopping to think, I prepared to pounce on him and capture him in the gunny sack just like a snipe hunt. Since he was pointed towards me with his squirters pointed the other way, I felt pretty safe. However, he did a cute little Olympic gymnastic handstand and raising his hind end high in the air, sprayed right up over his back and clobbered me square on my bare chest.

It's hard to explain the impact of a direct hit from a skunk. It is so strong you don't really smell it, rather you taste it. It burns your eyes and makes your nose run. Later on, when I was doing chemical warfare training during my time in the army, and enjoying the distinct sensation of tear gas, I was reminded of this incident some 13 years earlier. Since the damage had already been irreparably done, I proceeded to capture the skunk in the gunny sack. At that point in time Bob commented that," I guess I forgot to tell you it if you hold their tail down, they can't spray you." He tried not to laugh at my predicament. I couldn't figure out why he made me ride on the back of the pickup back out of the field. I tied the gunny sack to the handle bars of my bicycle and rode home. Mother was helpful in that she tossed me a bar of soap and said that the garden hose was available out in the backyard and the burn barrel was nearby. I scrubbed and scrubbed and scrubbed but it seemed like I only succeeded in spreading the stink around on the rest of my body.

When Dad came home from teaching a summer school class at the local university, we phoned our veterinarian Dr. Bert. He said, "Bring him on down and we'll get him descented."

When we got to his clinic he smiled and said, "I'm tempted to make you stay outside you smell so bad but you might want to watch and see what I'm going to do. There's no way I can find a vein on this little bugger but although it's not the recommended way, we can inject the anesthetic drug right into his body cavity where it will be absorbed." And no time the little skunk, who turned out to be a he, was breathing deeply and quietly on the surgery table. We neutered him and removed his two little stinker guns and the ammo sacs under his tail that contained the offending substance. We took him home and had to burn the gunny sack and my blue jeans. Fortunately, I had the rest of the summer to shed my stinky skin. That appeared to be the only way that I wasn't going to smell like a skunk indefinitely. In a month or so he learned to eat cat food and get along with our resident cats. My sister came up with the original name: Stinky. Just like a semi-wild skittish cat, however, he really didn't like to be caught and picked up, but once you had him caught, he resigned himself to sitting there nervously. However, as soon as he sensed the opportunity, he escaped. He was not proving to be a particularly desirable pet and we realized that he would have been much better off if we had left him to fend for himself as a wild animal. Would he have survived as an adolescent orphan? We asked Doc what to do not wanting to give up on Stinky. He said, "I have neutered and descended several skunks for Mrs. Jones through the years and she has a bunch of semi-domesticated and wild skunks that hang out on her back porch out by the river. Perhaps Stinky would like to join her family." And so, it came to pass.

That fall I visited Mrs. Jones to see how Stinky was doing. I must admit I was a little nervous knocking on her back-porch door surrounded by five black and white striped kitties looking for a hand out.

I never would have imagined that twenty years later I would be the guy using the drugs and the scalpel. Early in my career I descented a few skunks in a fully equipped outdoor barnyard surgery suite but eventually ceased doing it due to wildlife considerations and health risks. Fortunately, our Washington State skunks do not carry rabies, but pets brought in illegally from other areas can. It is, however, surprisingly prevalent in bats.

NOTE: Don't touch or capture bats, or spend time in bat habitat. Cautiously capture a bat only if there has been human contact so it can be tested for rabies.

ICELAND ADVENTURE

It was a worrisome juncture in my life. After 38 busy years as a practicing veterinarian, my body said it was finally time to retire, but I was a little concerned about how I was going to fill 10 to 12 hours of every day. I've never been very good at sitting still doing nothing. As much as I loved my challenging career, I realized this was finally an opportunity to do things totally unrelated to working with pets and livestock. It was time to work on my bucket list. So, for a total change of pace, why not an Iceland horse adventure. Horses, hair, brushes, saddles, stinky equipment, manure, insects, hoof picking, resetting shoes, working outside in the rain; what a total change-of-pace from the life of a veterinarian

Horses were brought to Iceland by the Norsemen in the ninth and tenth centuries. Prior to the modern industrial era, there were only three means of transportation to get around this island nation: by foot, by boat, or by horse. Self-driving electric automobiles weren't ready for market yet and Carnival Cruise Line hadn't expanded outside of the Caribbean. Due to stormy North Atlantic weather, boat travel was not always possible. Due to rugged terrain and long distances, foot travel was not particularly desirable or always practical. That left horses. They were rugged pony sized (13 hands) horses weighing only 700 to 850 pounds. They were tough, durable, and sure-footed but their size limited how far they could carry a person in a day. Thus, ancient Icelandic travelers brought along spare horses allowing them to switch mounts and travel all day long. And a summer day in Iceland could be 22 hours long.

This is the basis for the modern-day Icelandic Horseback Adventure. The Iceland Travel Association maintains 40 huts scattered along the ancient trails of the island. You ride for a week traveling each day to a different hut to spend the night but each rider has three horses. Two-thirds of the horses are traveling as a loose herd moving along with the horses ridden by the guests.

After a 10-hour 3500-mile flight to Reykjavik and a short introduction to the horses and the tack, we were on our way. Initially I grumbled quietly to myself saying, "This is not what I traveled and paid for." We were riding in a wide featureless ditch alongside a quiet two-lane highway. We were led by two of our guides and two thirds of the riders. Then came 35 loose horses and finally the one third of the remaining riders assisted by a guide. The job of the riders in front was to make sure the loose horses didn't escape on ahead, while the riders behind quietly herded loose straggling horses. The reason for the initial boring ride then became evident. There were pasture fences on one side, riders in front, and riders behind, and a quiet public highway on the other side. This allowed two vehicles, one in front of the herd and one behind the herd to help thus enabling complete herd containment as well as giving us time to learn how to travel with 35 loose horses.

And suddenly the adventure really began. We passed through an open gate and, as far as you could see, there was only brilliant green grass, beautiful blue lupines, coarse black basalt sand, jagged lava flows, and glacier covered mountains. There was not a fence to be seen, no trees, only a few birds, and distant white specks of widely scattered domestic sheep. There were no beer cans, fast food wrappers, or plastic grocery shopping bags either.

During that week we traveled 20 to 40 miles per day staying in a different hut every night. A truck traveled a more circuitous route bringing the cook, food, and our personal luggage. The scenery was beautiful in a uniquely stark sort of way. Things were basically black, white, and blue. Black sand, rocks, and mountain sides; white snow, birds, and clouds; and blue lakes, lupine flowers, and sometimes sky.

Fortunately, you're never too old to learn. And this was a learning opportunity for me to discover the qualities of the Icelandic horse. Much of the terrain is black course volcanic sand covered by relatively thin layers of lava. But lava does not completely cover the sand thus leaving dangerous jagged holes into which a horse could step. If the terrain was relatively smooth, we often let the horses spread out so that they could move freely as we traveled. In more rugged terrain all 50 horses traveled single file. Initially this was a little disconcerting because the horse you were riding might virtually bury his head in the bushy tail hair of the horse in front of him. You couldn't help but ask yourself: *How can my horse see where he is going*? When you observed more closely, you realize your horse put in his feet exactly the same place as the horse in front of him. As long as the horse at the beginning of this equine conga line could see what he was doing, the other horses only had to follow in his footsteps.

When the horses were traveling as a bunched-up herd, if you listened carefully, instead of hearing a random clip clop sound of their hooves striking the surface, you realized they were all *dancing to the same music.* These horses and their ancestors have been traveling through this rugged terrain as a herd for 11 centuries and have learned to travel as a relatively synchronized equine ballet.

The Icelandic horse has such a durable skin and thick hair coat, that no pads or blankets are required. English saddles are placed right on the horse's bare back, the girth is tightened, and off you ride for the next 2 or 3 hours.

A horse's head posture, eyes, and ears, communicate a lot to the rider about the horse's attitude and what it is thinking. The Icelandic ponies have a such thick bushy manes and forelocks that you can't see their eyes and only the tips of their ears show. Therefore, it is more difficult for the rider to interpret what the horse is trying to communicate.

Icelandics are a herd animal and have a definite pecking order. However, in our time with these 50 unique horses I did not see one horse kick, strike, or bite. If there were circumstances where one horse felt the need to show dominance over another, they lined up rump to rump and put it in reverse gear four-wheel drive full power. Squealing the whole time, one horse eventually conceded defeat and they went back to business as usual. I guess it could be compared to two strong guys arm wrestling instead of beating on each other. Perhaps one said to the other, "Butt out!"

Our head guide was one of three owners of this equine operation. He personally owned 450 horses When it was time to switch horses during the ride, we made a makeshift corral out of white tape with the loose horses bunched closely together inside. Our head guide would shoulder his way in among these 35 horses and catch the one which was to be your next riding partner. A bridle with a D ring snaffle bit was put on, and the horse was brought out underneath the tape, the saddle was switched to the new horse and the used horse was returned back to the herd. Within 20 minutes 17 horses had been caught, saddles switched, and we were remounted and on her way down the track into the Icelandic wilderness. We each carried rain gear tied on the back of our saddles. There was a constant dilemma of looking ahead at the incoming weather and deciding whether it would rain so hard that you needed the rain gear or whether you might be lucky and have the rain showers (or storm) miss you. Once you were underway, because there were 35 loose horses, you could not stop to put on rain gear if you had made the wrong initial choice. The only way to control all the animals was to keep them moving until they were hungry and there was a good grassy patch where they could all stop and graze.

At the end of each day we stopped at a different hut. It was just a small frame cabin where one wall was lined with bunk beds. There were usually two bathrooms and showers. One end of the cabin was the kitchen cooking area and the rest of the space was allocated to tables for socializing and eating. Each cabin had an adjacent corral where large round bales of hay had been repositioned. Once the horses were located in the corral and enough hay had been distributed, we retreated to the cabin where everybody had a chance to shower and change in to clean dry clothes. Soon every place where wet clothes could possibly be hung was draped with wet horsey smelling clothing. We sat and chatted while drinking coffee, tea, and hot chocolate. The cook, with a few of us to assist, was soon preparing our dinner meal. There could be locally produced chicken, pork or beef, sometimes horse steaks, and always cod fish. My memories of eating cod at home back in the States were that it was rather bland and tasteless. What we ate in Iceland was a delicious, rich, and savory food that we looked forward to with our dinner meal.

Iceland is blessed with a very small flying insect call a midge. They spend most of their existence in a larval form feeding on organic matter in the soil. Their adult breeding final stage lasts only a few days. During the short summer months there is apparently a hatch of midges going on somewhere in Iceland most of the time. If you are unlucky enough to be where a hatch is ongoing, your life can be pretty miserable for a few days. They don't bite or cause any pain or diseases but they are so thick as to even obscure your vision. They are everywhere. They get in your eyes, your nose, your ears, and your mouth. They get under your eyelashes in your hair and everywhere. They can even get under your eyelids. *They are not fair. They do not care. They get in your hair. They are everywhere.* Doctor Seuss should write a poem about them. But they don't bite. Nevertheless, you can imagine if these hatches lasted longer, they could drive you a little bit batty (or buggy). You could sometimes look off into the near distance and see thick clouds of flying midges moving around like a murmuration of Starlings We were encouraged to buy fly masks which, when we encountered an ongoing hatch, were indispensable. You would lift a corner of the mask to get food underneath to eat. Otherwise, you were guaranteed to consume a half a dozen high protein low cholesterol midges with almost every bite of food. They somehow got into the huts and spent time flying around the windows looking for an escape. There could be a pile of dead midges half an inch thick at the bottom of each of the windows. The fisheries people had observed that lakes which had more frequent hatches of midges had fish which grew faster and fatter than lakes where no hatch had occurred. The midges impact fish, birds, and even vegetation near any permanent water.

The horses didn't seem to be bothered by the midges. Their bushy manes and forelocks kept them out of their eyes and ears but they did seem to snort a little more perhaps trying to keep them out of their noses.

The footing was too abrasive for a barefoot horse to carry a rider so all the horses were shod. With 50 horses traveling long distances each day, one was sure to lose a shoe so the guide carried a few basic farrier's tools. There were no trees or posts to tie to so he used his own saddle horse for an anchor post. The horse needing a shoe was attached to a heavy leather strap around the guide's horse to secure it while a new shoe was put on. The other guides rode younger relatively untrained horses thus preparing them for eventual use by the guests.

Atlantic storms frequently arrive from the west and we awoke one morning to a black threatening sky. Our guide admitted it was likely to be a cold wet miserable day in the saddle and that rather than stop for lunch he recommended that we just keep riding to the next hut. We switched horses 5 or 6 times and traveled 38 miles in about 6 hours.

The Icelandic horse has a unique gait called the tolt, which is described as a four-beat running walk. Unlike the trot, where the whole horse's body is launched momentarily into the air, the tolt always has one foot planted solidly on the ground producing a less bouncy smoother ride.

During that week, 4 men and 13 northern European ladies shared bathrooms, bedrooms, and dressing rooms. For the men, it was prudent when getting up in the morning or when getting ready for bed at night, to keep your eyes averted from the end of the hut where the ladies were dressing. Similalrly, there were often no bushes or rocks to hide behind when it was time for a **rest break**. Occasional flashes of white flesh indicated it was time to politely gaze off at the opposite far horizon until all the ladies had returned from their excursion. Everybody spoke English but there is enough similarity between Norwegian, Finish, and Icelandic that they could communicate. Two of our guides had been previous guests who loved the adventure so much that they spent their vacation time as unpaid staff just to be there.

What were the highlights of this week of horseback riding? I rode 14 different Icelandic horses in an unfamiliar English saddle. We rode through dense clouds of midges and hock deep peat moss bogs. We traversed melting snowfields which threatened to collapse beneath you and rode around exposed egg filled golden plover nests. We saw strange looking multi-patterned sheep, forded milky white boot filling glacial melt rivers, and explored ancient stone huts now covered only by rusty sheet-metal. We consumed quarts of oatmeal porridge covered in blue berries and drowned in rich Icelandic cream. We saw wings of honking Graylag geese. We saw mirrored mountain reflections in milky-white glacier-fed lakes only marked by the dimples rising fish feeding on the hatching midges. There were valleys totally carpeted in all the shades of blue from the lupins. The base of the flower cluster was a deep indigo and the color transitioned through violets, blues, pinks to the tip where the white blossoms looked like they were frosted with a light snow. On the last day a glorious sun appeared and as we lounged in its radiant heat someone jokingly said, "I'm sure glad I brought my sunscreen".

If you have any interest in just watching, learning about, or riding an Icelandic horse in Iceland, look up Eldhestar (volcano horses). Hourly, half day, all day, 3-day and 7-day lessons and tours are offered for all levels of riding skill.

ICELAND NATURAL HISTORY

The Iceland Island had trees a thousand years ago but the settlers totally stripped landscape of anything taller than a bush. There are now, however, areas of significant reforestation with plantations of rapidly growing Austrian Pines. 3000 years ago, the coastal plains were covered by birch forests but the Norse settlers used slash-and-burn techniques to clear fields for oats, barley, and pasture for horses and sheep. The few trees remaining were used for building and to feed their forges. 25% of the land used to be forested but there is now only about 1% that has been reclaimed by tree plantations. It is assumed that the settlers totally deforested Iceland in about three centuries. The thin loose soil was then exposed to the erosive forces of water and wind. It is very difficult to reestablish vegetation because the gale force winds can literally rip trees and clumps of grass right out of the ground. 40% of Iceland is what is called a wet desert. There is rainforest quantity of rain but the erosive forces of wind and water make it exceedingly difficult for vegetation to get established. Aspen trees have been planted but the wandering sheep love to eat Aspen. The strikingly blue lupine is actually an introduced plant. In attempts to stabilize the soil, first grass is planted and later lupine is introduced as it is a nitrogen fixing plant. Eventually enough soil is stabilized that trees can be planted. Initially, slow-growing birches are planted and eventually Sitka spruce, Lodgepole pine, and Black cottonwood can take root. All these trees initially came from Alaska where similar conditions exist. Now, everything is propagated in geothermal heated greenhouses since it is illegal to bring any vegetation into Iceland. These trees grow three times faster in Alaska than in Iceland. Trees planted in Iceland 80 years ago her now only 40 to 50 ft tall. They would be 150 ft tall in Alaska

Only birds and Arctic fox are native. Everything else was introduced by Norse settlers. Selective breeding of livestock led to animals best adapted to the harsh environment. The Icelandic Sheep dog is of Spitz breeding and looks much like a Samoyed except its wool coat shades from white to tan to brown to black. The Icelandic sheep is horned and can shade from white to black or be multicolored like a Holstein cow. They were able to survive extremely harsh winters protected by their heavy wool coat. They provided wool for weaving fabric, skins, and milk for cheese and other dairy products. Having been isolated for thousands of years, the livestock of Iceland are vulnerable to diseases found elsewhere in the world. Therefore, no live animals can be introduced to the island which is free of most animal diseases, particularly tuberculosis and brucellosis, Rodents such as mice and rats have followed human settlements. Escaped mink prey on native bird nests. Introduced reindeer are semi-wild populations controlled to preserve precious grazing land. Pet rabbits and hares have been released and become a plague on the vegetation in some areas. Traditionally, pastures were community-owned and the sheep were allowed to graze at will on these community assets. In the fall, the owners work together to collect and bring sheep into winter paddocks They travel on foot or horseback aided by their unique Icelandic Sheepdogs. Once all the animals are found, they are put in a corral shaped like the spokes of a wheel to be sorted into the individual flocks and taken home to be fed until spring grass is again available and the sheep are turned out to forage on their own. Icelandic inheritance law divides property amongst family heirs upon an owner's death so title to a parcel of property can be complex with numerous owners and ownership of large parcels difficult to obtain. Rent for pasture may have to be portioned out among multiple owners

More horses exist outside Iceland, (100,000) than inside (80,000). There is one horse for every four Icelandic residents. Livestock, and horses in particular, can leave Iceland but no animals can be brought into the island to protect the health and bloodlines of unique Icelandic breeds. Obviously, the best horses are retained in Iceland and not exported elsewhere in the world. Iceland is self-sufficient in meat, dairy, and poultry, and eggs for its population of 337,000. Most of these products are produced just as they are in the United States under confined factory farm conditions. The breeds of horses, cattle, sheep, goats, and dogs are unique to Iceland and in many cases trace back genetically to animals from a thousand years ago. Only 1% of the land mass is cultivated. They have learned to cultivate forage crops which mature very quickly during their short summers. Iceland's grass is especially nutritious and grows very rapidly in the 22 hours of sunlight. Fortunately, the need for chemicals is limited since insect pests struggle to survive in this harsh environment.

Harvested forage is wrapped in white plastic which prevents exposure to oxygen. Like silage, the available oxygen is consumed and then only bacteria which can grow in the absence of oxygen turns the hay into haylage. When these bags of haylage are opened, it smells like opening a can of sauerkraut.)

Iceland sits atop the Mid-Atlantic Ridge where the Eurasian and North America tectonic plates diverge at a rate of about one inch a year. It is essentially a giant volcanic island. Its location in the northern latitudes and in the middle of the Gulf Stream make it a place of snow and ice. It is truly a land of **Fire and Ice**

Visit Iceland soon before it is totally transformed by tourism.

THE STOCKING CAP

Sue always wanted a dog. Not just any dog. A big dog. In fact, a very big white dog. She had graduated with a degree in accounting but, due to student loan payments, had only been able to afford a small no-pets-allowed apartment. Finally, after attaining some professional success as a financial advisor, it was time to move up; to a bigger studio apartment and to a big white dog.

A Great Pyrenees had always been her dream. After communicating with several breeders and checking into blood lines and pedigrees, she picked out a soccer ball sized bundle of white fluff with a handle on the back end. Bounder was eagerly transported to Sue's *spacious* apartment. It was soon evident that the apartment was not really as *spacious* as she had thought. As quickly as she collected and returned Bounder's toys to the box, he emptied them back out again. When she organized the shoes in her closet, he reorganized them all over the apartment. Chew toys were not nearly as much fun as fuzzy slippers. Water dishes were more fun play in rather than to drink from and couches were much more comfortable than dog beds. Somehow, Sue somehow survived Bounder's adolescence. Obedience classes, play dates with other dogs, and long walks around the city and countryside filled her spare time and greatly enriched her life.

Great Pyrenees are big white *very hairy* dogs. They don't really live with you; they graciously allow you to reside with them. There is long white hair everywhere so the only thing to do is acquire light colored carpeting and like colored furniture. If your house accessories are a dark color, white hair becomes exceedingly conspicuous. You don't need dental floss because your food comes equipped with it. Sue was a very conscientious pet owner and she made sure her dog was well fed, well groomed, and well exercised. This necessitated almost daily grooming and vacuuming, and thus shopping bags full of white dog hair.

Sue's talents extended beyond accounting and she was immersed in spinning and weaving with various textiles to create works of art. She had the brilliant idea to see if Bounder's hair could be spun into fibers that could be used for weaving. The dog hair was a little slippery, so spinning it into strands required special processing and technique, but Sue persisted and triumphed. Eventually, she had a sizable yarn ball of Great Pyrenees white dog hair. Now what? Her grandmother had taught her how to knit, so Sue decided to make herself a white stocking cap for use during the colder winter season. She stopped in from time to time to tell us of her progressing weaving endeavor.

Finally, she said that she had completed her project and wanted to show her work to all the office staff. We expected her to come in about noon on her lunch break after we had completed our morning appointments. It had been a moderately warm humid morning. In fact, it had rained pretty hard for a few minutes late in morning. We were all sitting round in the treatment area recovering from an unusually busy Saturday morning when we heard the front door of the reception area open. There was a rush of fresh air through the open door and someone commented, "Wow! Something certainly smells Doggie.

Cindy went to the front office to greet whoever had entered. She shouted back to us, "Sue is here to show off her new hat." We all trooped out to the front room.

Someone said, "Where is Bounder? It certainly smells like wet dog in here."

There was a stricken look on Sue's face when she said, "Bounder isn't here. He's on a playdate out at his boarding kennel."

There was an embarrassing moment of silence when we realized that it was Sue's wet dog hair knitted hat that smelled. In spite of carefully cleaning and carding, Bounders recycled long hair still smelled like *wet dog hair*. On her next visit Sue, with a chagrined look on her face, explained that her carefully fabricated hat, after having been sprayed multiple times with Febreze, found a place of honor on the hat rack near her apartment front door. It was definitely not allowed to go out for walks in the rain.

KILLER

Training to be a veterinarian was hard work. Or was it? First, it was a major accomplishment just to gain admission to the WSU College of Veterinary Medicine. The curriculum wasn't really that difficult: there was just lots of it. You had to learn and often memorize vast quantities of information and data, a lot of which you might never use again. Quite a bit of it was actually boring but it was necessary background for becoming a veterinarian. Was it work? Well some of it was. A lot of the book learning part seemed like work. But finally, you got to the part that you knew was going to be important for your eventual career: learning how to do procedures and tests which would become part of your everyday routine. And then there were the labs and surgeries where you actually got to practice these skills. I made the conscious decision to not spend too much time on information I thought I would never see again, but to learn very thoroughly the information that would be useful and make me a better practitioner. This filled most of the hours in a day for four years until eventual graduation.

But some breaks in this routine were needed to maintain a minimal level of sanity. My wife and I did quite a bit local traveling to explore, to go on picnics and excursions, and to go camping if weather and time allowed. We explored the back roads and canyons of the Snake River country. We drove off into the vast rolling wheat fields to prowl around abandoned old barns, and we drove up into the Moscow Mountain to go picnicking, berry picking, and camping. My wife was always careful to pack some Oreo Cookies. On one of these exploratory drives when we were returning back to our small rented house in Pullman, WA., we saw a brightly colored object fluttering weakly alongside the road. We stopped to investigate and were able to identify it as an American Kestrel. Its back was rufous colored with dark bands on the tops of the wings. The top of its head had beautiful bluish tones. It didn't seem to be injured but was just weak and unable to fly more than a few feet. Being an enthusiastic veterinary student, I decided that the bird needed to be rescued and we took it home with us. It gobbled down moist cat food and seemed to get significantly stronger on through the rest of the weekend. On Monday morning, I took it into the College of Veterinary Medicine where we had a professor who specialized in birds, their diseases, care, and rehabilitation. Dr. Eric examined the bird and confirmed that it was a male American Kestrel, and that it was a young bird that had not been successful enough hunting to maintain a bodyweight sufficient to fly. That's why we found it on the ground too weak to escape and care for itself. Kestrels are native to much of the western hemisphere and are a small falcon about the size of a mourning dove. This little bird was hospitalized and thus provided an opportunity for students to examine and care for a small wild falcon. In about three weeks he had gained significant weight and was even able to catch large flying insects that we released into its aviary. Nevertheless, its future survival was uncertain. I had a friend, Jerry, who was a licensed falconer and who flew a red-tailed hawk, a peregrine falcon, and a prairie falcon.

We sometimes did outings with him for the pure joy of working with the birds. He had a Britany Spaniel named Daisy who was part of the team. Daisy would hunt and locate birds or small mammals on the ground. The falcons or hawk flew high in the air or perched in a tree to watch her. When the dog located game, the predator birds would literally dive into action. It was an awesome sight to see the bird from high elevation attacking prey on or rising up from the ground. If the hunt was successful there was a collision as the falcon or hawk created a puff of feathers or cloud of dust.

This was the environment our young Kestrel, who ultimately acquired the name Killer, would call his home. All of Jerry's free time was dedicated to the training, care, and flying of his birds. The trick and skill of the falconer is to keep his bird healthy enough to be a strong flyer by carefully watching its weight and quality of its plumage but at the same time hungry enough to hunt. Killer had been receiving some indoor training but it was uncertain that, if he was taken outside, he could be recaptured or if he would just fly off into the wild with his survival uncertain. We collected moths and grasshoppers and other large flying insects and released them in Jerry's borrowed old barn falconry mew so Killer could practice his hunting techniques. Jerry had a roommate who was a student lab technician and was thus able to have an income to help meet his educational expenses. Consequently, there was an underground supply of juvenile unneeded male laboratory mice for killer to further hone his survival skills. For Killer, I guess it was a little like shooting fish in a barrel.

My wife and I, being Killer's rescuers and defacto supporters, were invited for the day of Killer's first hunt outing. We loaded our picnic basket with some cheap wine, some artisan bread and cheese, and a small barbecue to prepare our wieners. Kestrels are fascinating to watch as they hunt. They can perch in a tree or face into a light breeze and actually hover in place; not quite as well as a hummingbird but nevertheless long enough to observe insects, small rodents, and even smaller birds which might become their next meal.

The trip was a success in that when Killer was released, he flew and circled and hunted, and came, as he had been trained to do, back to the human hand which was protected by a light leather glove. He was not, however, able to document any kills. My wife and I were friends with Jerry and his girlfriend as well as his roommate, the lab technician, and his wife, who were from Texas. About three weeks later we were invited over for some Texas chicken BBQ. Just inside the door of the house that the foursome rented was a cork bulletin board. I happened to glance at the bulletin board as we entered the house. There, prominently displayed, front and center, carefully attached by four blue thumbtacks, was a very small mouse hide. There was a very small tag attached to this trophy. It said "Killer's first kill. October 13th 1973." Jerry released Killer to the wild on a warm spring day the following May. He had become a successful hunter and had matured into a handsome brightly colored male American Kestrel falcon. We were confident that he would be able to woo a young female Kestrel and surely, they would live happily ever after hunting as a team to raise many small broods of successful hunters.

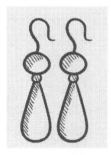

SPECIAL GIFTS

Hobbies are supposed to be good for the mind, the soul, and body. George was a mechanical engineer but his hobby was jewelry creation. He made rings, bracelets, necklaces, pins, earrings, and almost anything else. He was self-employed and when between jobs he liked to keep busy with this interesting sideline. He had lost his wife to cancer a few years earlier and the kids had graduated, married, and were producing grandchildren. He preferred custom items but many of the basic components for jewelry manufacturing could be purchased from hobby shops and all that the hobbyist had to do was to find interesting stones and objects for the centerpiece. Thus, George was always on the lookout for colorful or semi-precious stones to incorporate into his work. He like to hike and, in the process, had amassed a significant collection of petrified wood, blue agates, jade, and quartz. He always had a couple of rock tumblers going and had mastered the art of cutting stones with diamond blade tools. He had also been working on perfecting the lost wax casting technique and used go to junk stores and estate sales to find good deals on old gold jewelry. Using a tiny crucible, he would pour the heated molten gold into a hole in a mold thus forming the rough shape of a piece of jewelry.

A big old farmhouse is a pretty quiet place when you have a family of one. Feeling the need for a companion, George went to the animal shelter looking for housemate. There happened to be a Golden cocker spaniel there who had not been a good fit for a family since their house was empty for eight hours of the day. Thus, they had released the dog to the animal shelter in hopes that a better situation could be found. The result was double good fortune; good fortune that the dog found a caring loving home, and that a person found a loving caring pet. George and Daisy bonded immediately. We saw Daisy from time to time at our veterinary hospital for vaccinations, some dental work, and recurring skin and ear infections. One fall George brought Daisy in, explaining that she needed to urinate frequently and if she had an accident, as cocker spaniels are sometimes known to do, there was a slight tinge of red in the urine.

You can gently squeeze on a dog or cat's belly and locate the urinary bladder. If the bladder is empty you would not be able to find it but if it were urine filled or had some other structure inside, it was easy to locate. When we gently squeezed Daisy's bladder, there was a distinct sensation of rocks inside a cloth sack. An x-ray confirmed the diagnosis that Daisy had cystic calculi or bladder stones. Digestive metabolic processes in some dogs can result in urine salts that crystalize into hard stones consisting mainly of calcium. Hypothetically, using a very specialized diet, it is possible to dissolve these stones. But success is marginal and the only realistic approach is surgery to open the bladder and remove the stones. When you determine the chemical nature of the stones you can then adjust the dog's diet to prevent stones from forming in the future.

So, Daisy came back the next day for her cystotomy; cyst referring to bladder, and otomy referring to opening up. We anesthetized her, shaved the golden hair off of her soft belly and scrubbed her carefully for surgery. An incision was made through the skin and midline allowing us to insert fingers through the incision and retrieve her urinary bladder. It popped out through the opening and sat there smiling at us like small golden water balloon. An incision was made through the wall of the urinary bladder and out rolled half a dozen marble-sized stones on to the surgical drapes. We zipped up the bladder, closed the peritoneum and facia, and put a careful row of sutures down the incision in the skin. Later that day, when she had recovered from the anesthesia, we took her on a slow walk outside to the canine outdoor public bathroom. She tottered out and sniffed around a little bit, squatted, and produced a beautiful stream of light amber colored liquid.

When George came to retrieve Daisy the following morning, we asked him, "Do you want these stones?"

He replied, "Let me take a look at them."

When he examined them, he said, "There must be something I can do with these strange little things. I know! I'll make a pendant and some earrings." And he did.

About three weeks later George came in the front door late in the afternoon with a big smile on his face. "I've got something to show you all," he said. He pulled out a small black velvet jewelry box from his coat pocket, opened it, and laid out three small items on the reception room counter. There was a pair of earrings with the stones hanging on a short link of chain and a similar pendant with a larger stone suspended from a chain. The chain was gold and made a striking contrast to the dark bronze color of the stones. For the three items he had chosen appropriately sized stones that we had retrieved from Daisey's bladder. They had been cut and polished into a tear drop shape. The stones were made up of concentric light and dark areas kind of like an onion or the cross grain of a tree. They were rather actually rather attractive. My associate Mary didn't actually wear much jewelry but agreed to model these items. They looked rather nice in contrast to the dark green of her surgical scrubs. We chatted for a while and then George left. He said, with a strange cryptic smile on his face, "I hope you like them and I think you'll be surprised by the comments you get when you wear them."

We got pretty busy on through the afternoon and finally when the rush was over, we sat down for a short break. With a quizzical expression on her face, Dr. Mary asked, "Is there a mess back in the kennel room that needs to be cleaned up? I keep getting a strong odor of dog pee."

Someone went back and checked and said, "No everything is clean and odorless back there." Suddenly it dawned on us. As Dr. Mary had been wearing the jewelry it warmed up to body temperature and began to exude the odor a dog pee. At first there were a few giggles and then out right laughs.

Someone said, "Now we know what George meant when he said that we would be surprised at the comments after we wore the jewelry."

Mary said, "I rather like the looks of them but the stink would make them impossible to wear at any place other than a veterinary clinic or dog kennel. They might be good for a bad blind date however"

Some suggestions were made such as: "Only wear it on a cold day, just wear it when the wind is blowing, or that they might be appropriate if you ever judged a dog show." Mary did try the more practical suggestion of painting them with something to seal the surface. After applying half a dozen layers of clear nail polish, they actually became semi acceptable. Mary did wear them occasionally except not on warm humid days when the faint odor could still be distinguished.

BOSQUE BOY

At least it was a beautiful Indian summer day. There had been frost on the lawn that morning but the day had warmed up to almost shorts and tee shirt temperature. However, there wasn't too much else to be happy about. I had just put down a horse that was arguably the best cow cutting horse ever to graze in Kittitas County.

The owner and I both got misty-eyed. We had had a good long heartfelt conversation about the horse, his personality, and his accomplishments beforehand. Assisted by the steady calloused hands of the owner, I had injected a large lethal overdose of an anesthetic into the horse's jugular vein. He stood there quietly and calmly for about 30 seconds took one last deep sighing breath and collapsed heavily to the ground. I took out my stethoscope to check for a heartbeat and the owner walked a short distance away to collect himself. I saw his shoulders give a short brief shutter and watched his gaze shift from the ground to the far-off sagebrush covered foothills. The back of his hand was lifted briefly to his face. I too had to stand and walk a short distance away. After a minute or two we both returned and look down at the lifeless body of a previously magnificent horse. We didn't speak as we shook hands one last time and each returned to his respective truck.

Word Hobbs had been a New Mexico cattle rancher who also broke and trained horses, especially cow cutting horses. He purchased the young black colt for a friend in 1961 and when the time came also broke the horse and started him on cow cutting training.

A cow cutting horse is truly something special. Horseman say that such a horse has *a lot of cow* in him. Just like a good bird hunting dog, cow cutting horses instinctively anticipate the cattle's movement in attempting to rejoin the herd and truly enjoy what they are doing. The rider only helps the horse to select one cow from the middle of the herd and later another one from the periphery and, using only leg cues, assist the horse in its two-and-a-half-minute cutting session.

Before the days of modern cattle handling equipment, if an animal needed attention, it had to be isolated from the herd, maybe driven to another corral or pasture, or perhaps roped. A cutting horse truly loved the wild dodging back and forth to prevent an isolated cow from returning to the herd. Horseman love to show and brag about their horses and cow cutters are no exception. The first known organized cow cutting competition was held in Haskell, Texas in 1898 with indoor competitions held in 1908 at Ft. Worth. In1918 the Fort Worth Stock Show had the first indoor rodeo, which included the first cow cutting competition in conjunction with a rodeo. In 1946 the National Cutting Horse Association was formally organized.

Ward eventually bought Bosky Boy, who had proven to be too quick and athletic for his owner. It's not much fun to be unceremoniously dumped off your horse in front of an audience at a cow cutting competition. Ward used him for a routine ranch work as well as cow cutting competitions. When Ward moved to the Ellensburg area in 1969, Bosque Boy, of course, came along and performed for the first time at the Saturday night cow cutting competition at the Ellensburg Rodeo.

I saw Bosky Boy work cattle several times doing late 80s and even though he was an old man, he was still a tremendous crowd-pleaser. He would lay his ears flat, bare his teeth, and his body language and sheer determination would almost intimidate an unfortunate cow. Ward had to be a good rider and have a mind on the same wave length as his horse just to stay in the saddle. There is no embarrassment in hanging on to the saddle horn to keep from being unseated.

Time has a way of catching up with man and beast and as Bosque Boy approached his mid-twenties arthritis began to set in. He had a private summertime pasture reserved just for him and in the winter had his own deep bedded stall in the barn. But in the summer of 1989, it was obvious that getting around was painful and the only thing he could do under those circumstances was to lie down to rest his aching joints. However, gradually increasing weakness made it difficult for him to get back up. Bosque Boy wasn't a heavy horse so, on some occasions, Ward needed to call his son or a neighbor to help give Bosky Boy a boost to get back on his feet. However, this is not much of a life for a horse and the sad day finally arrived.

Ward had said that time and the cold Ellensburg winter weather were catching up on him too so he had decided to move back to New Mexico to finish out his cattlemen's days under more hospitable temperatures. He said, "I know some of my friends around here would laugh if they heard me say this, but I just don't have the heart to have him just hauled away or buried up here. Is there a way we can have him cremated so I can take his ashes back to New Mexico where he was born, raised, and trained?

I said, "I'll find a way to get that done, Ward!"

A FISH STORY

George and Jenny had retired after long diligent careers working for local city government. George shaved at least once a week and sported a scraggly grey ponytail. Jenny was always carefully dressed and had short stylish hair that highlighted her blue eyes and high cheekbones. As a city clerk, Jenny drove a desk and as a maintenance worker, George often drove a backhoe. Jenny had collected, and piled paperwork and George had collected and piled dirt. Thus, there were many similarities between their two jobs. Now that they had free time on their hands, there were few things they enjoyed more than going fishing at the nearby freeway ponds. The fishing was the most important part; the catching was a purely secondary benefit. In fact, if the catching was poor, the fishing was still great and there were no smelly fish to clean. They would set up a sun canopy, securely staked down in case the wind picked up, and of course brought along their two best friends. One was Blondie, a retired yellow lab who liked to sleep in the shade under the truck or beside the lawn chair or cooler. The other was Mister Stubbs, a large Manx tabby who was definitely not retired and was still young and inquisitive. He liked to prowl along the banks of the pond looking for frogs, insects, and small rodent to ambush in the cattails and bushes. Anything that moved got his full attention. He never strayed far and when they called, he came bounding back not wanting to miss out on any action or the next scheduled meal. Often, he returned with fresh table meat: a vole, deer mouse, and even rats weighing a third as much as he did.

Mister Stubbs liked to entertain George and Jenny by chasing a laser light all over the house. If they tired of this game, he would force them to play fetch with him by chasing a small rolled up wad of paper when they threw it. If they tired of even this game, then he would ambush Blondie's tail. He would wait patiently until she dozed off and then pounce on her tail. He was at least careful not to use his claws in this game. Eventually, she had learned, when she remembered, to tuck her tail safely underneath when she needed a nap. George told Jenny that, "The reason Mister Stubbs attacks Blondie's tail is because he has *tail envy*. He doesn't have one of his own."

All four of them were waiting for me for my first appointment on a Monday morning. George was dressed in his Sunday best: a Seahawks tee shirt and freshly washed bib overalls and Jenny in her retirement uniform: jeans and a sweatshirt that said on the front, "*Women can tell fish stories too.*" They explained that they had been fishing the previous Saturday and had decided to take a short nap in the warm afternoon breeze. They were startled awake by the ringing of the bell on their spare fishing pole. When they looked to see what they had caught they discovered that there was a large hairy tabby Manx catfish on the other end of the line. Apparently, there had been a cluster of salmon eggs left on the hook and Mister Stubbs couldn't resist the proffered bait.

What to do? Well first they had to convince him to stop fighting and let them gather him up. It didn't long take long to discover that the line disappeared right down his throat. Gentle cautious tugging accomplished nothing so the only recourse was to cut the line and hope for the best. They decided to take a wait-and-see attitude and hope that everything would pass on through in the usual and accustomed fashion. Catching had been slow anyway, so they finished their Busch beer and packed up the cooler and canopy in the back of their half ton Chevy and went home to watch the Mariners baseball game while keeping Mister Stubbs inside under careful observation. However, when the alarm went off on Monday morning, Mister Stubbs was in obvious distress and had several inches of 10lb fishing line protruding from the end opposite from his mouth.   Again, gentle tugging accomplished nothing and George and Jenny brought him in for an early morning visit. An x-ray indicated that Mister Stubbs indeed had his panties in a bunch. We could see on the X-ray, and palpate with our fingers, tightly coiled areas of intestines in an abnormal pattern. There was no sign of the fishhook, however. The only option was to go spelunking in Mister Stubbs' belly to see if we could rectify his circumstances. Some *doctor feelgood* got him resting quietly and ready for an emergency surgery later that morning. During the lunch hour we shaved all the hair off his belly and opened him up.

Imagine a laundry bag with a drawstring which gathers up and closes one end. In Mister Stubbs case, the drawstring was the fish line, and the laundry bag was Mister Stubbs entire digestive tract. What should have been eight feet long was gathered up into a one-foot cluster. Ultimately, we made five small incisions to explore his intestinal tract and, in each case, we were able to discover the fish line inside and retrieve the downstream portion. Eventually, we even had to make a small incision in his stomach and were able to retrieve what we thought was the last remaining segments of fish line. However, when we tugged on the fish line going upstream somebody noticed some slight mechanical twitching in the area of the Mister Stubbs' throat. Feeling rather foolish I asked my surgical assistant to check in the Mister Stubbs' mouth. Sure enough, there was the fish hook still with one salmon egg attached, firmly hooked in the area near his tonsils.

Someone said, "Wouldn't it have been easier to have discovered the hook first and just pulled it back out the way it came in?"

I said sheepishly. "Certainly, that could have been true." However, we realized that once we got looking around inside the kitty it was obvious that we had lucked out and had taken the proper approach. Pulling from the fish hook end might have drawn the fish line back out again but most certainly would have resulted in cutting through the intestinal wall making things considerably and potentially fatally worse. Needless to say, owners and veterinarians *hate it when that happens*

We patched up all the little holes we had made in his digestive tract with neat little sutures. Would you believe that the suture material is called *cat gut*? Cat gut is actually carefully prepared thread made from the muscle layer of sheep's intestine. No, we didn't kill the fatted lamb but relied on companies that work with other companies that traditionally supply lamb chops and Easter leg of lamb.

Mister Stubbs went home the next day with instructions to give him small frequent feedings of soft food and restricted activity for one week. We, of course, admonished them to keep loaded fishing weapons carefully secured from small children and cats. Two weeks later they brought him in for a quick *lab test and a cat sca*n. The results were favorable and we further documented his attitude by flashing a laser pen light on the floor. Blondie kept her tail carefully tucked out of reach. George and Jenny promised to bring in some fresh fish from their next trip in partial payment for my treatment of Mister Stubbs.

CHARLOTTE

Charlotte's career began as Brenda Webb's 4-H project. Weaner piglets are selected, fed, and raised with meticulous record keeping, shown at the county fair, and then sent off to be prepared for IHOP breakfast menus or western barbecue enjoyment. The Webb girls had grown up loving the story of Charlotte's Web but perhaps had forgotten that Charlotte was the spider and Wilbur was the pig. So, I guess you could say that Charlotte was named after a spider. When the time came after the county fair for pigs to be sent off to market, Brenda just couldn't bear to see her friend Charlotte sent off to such an ignominious fate. So, she had tearfully petitioned her parents for some other alternative. Thus, that fall Charlotte was introduced to a Wilbur look alike for a romantic interlude and the saga began. It takes a pig a little less than 4 month to produce a whole assembly of little future sausages. She can produce two litters year with as many as 12:to 14 in a litter. ***This is why it is extremely important to*** *carefully control the breeding of pigs for otherwise they would soon overrun the world.* Think "Planet of the Apes" only with pigs.

Brenda and the Webbs read all the literature about breeding, feeding, and farrowing pigs and had everything ready for the big event in mid-February. Based on counting the days on the calendar, the fact that Charlotte was a little swollen behind, and the fact that she was leaking milk, the Webbs were pretty sure that the magic moment was imminent. They had called me for some last-minute instructions I told them that ninety-nine times out of a hundred everything proceeded quite happily and uneventfully. Charlotte was unlikely to fall into that 1% category.

Once sows get down to the business of birthing, they stop eating and lie down on their sides. The whole process may take only about 2 hours with another new piglet popping out as often as every 10 to 15 minutes. Amazingly, the piglets seem to know which way to turn. If they turn the right way, they will find an inviting nipple awaiting their arrival. Should they do a left turn, they wind up in no man's land on the dark side of the moon. They always seem to make the right decision where they latch onto a nipple which they will personally own for the rest of their nursing life. This is where the phrase *a bum TEET* comes from, because not every mammary gland produces adequate milk and some pigs will be smaller having a reduced food supply at the family buffet.

But back to Charlotte and her intimate problems. Everything was ready but nothing was happening. The Webbs knew that Charlotte was in labor but was not producing any pigs. So about 1 in the morning I got a frantic call. I was not on call but they apologized and explained, "We called all the other veterinarians and they all conveniently said they didn't work on pigs. We are really desperate. Can you please come and help us?" None of our local group of veterinarians had much, if any, experience with pigs but I had had some exposure during my training so after I woke up and managed to turn my brain on, I said I would be right over.

We didn't have self-driving cars in those days so I actually had to keep my eyes on the road as I made first tracks in the lightly falling snow. The Webbs had a nice clean straw bedded pen in the garage for Charlotte. The family car was outside disappearing under the new snow. She was almost buried in a pile of deep straw and grunted quietly as I approached. There was a heat lamp, a pile of freshly laundered towels in an old bassinette, and a bucket of steaming water. A quick examination seemed to indicate that Charlotte was not sick. Her temperature, respiration, and circulation seem to be normal but there were no little pigs coming down the chute. The medical term we use is dystocia. It can be caused by uterine inertia where the uterine contractions don't seem to get properly started or continue in a coordinated fashion. Imagine the complexity of the situation. If there are 12 pigs lined up and the uterus starts pushing them all out at once, by the time the last one is delivered the placenta would have long since been detached and the piglet would surely be dead. Somehow, miraculously, the uterus contracts and such a way as to push them out one at a time thus maintaining the umbilical lifelines until the last one is delivered.

The only thing to do is to scrub the momma pig's behind and coat your arm with appropriate lubrication and reach into this long warm dark birth tunnel to see, I mean feel, what is going on. The first pig did seem to be a little larger than normal and this is what perhaps what upset the normal course of events. Piglets can come out back feet first or snout first even with the front legs folded back along the chest. This pig was head first so I was able to grasp its head with my fingers and by tugging and tugging gently, coax it on out into the bright cold world. Everybody cheered when it took a few quick gasping breaths and proceeded to totter around to the appropriate side where, within minutes, it began nursing. We all thought that that would solve the problem and sat back expecting more pigs to be delivered shortly. We waited and waited and waited, but nothing happened. I'm not sure if the cliché *A Watched Pot Never Boils* was appropriate but someone said anyway it and Charlotte just grunted. At that point we administered a drug called oxytocin which encourages uterine contractions. Charlotte seemed to grunt indicating she was having more labor pains and uterine contraction but nothing else happened. So, another long reach into the warm slippery tunnel and guess what I found? Amazingly, it was another pig! This one was coming back feet first. And so, it continued 10 more times, until as best we could tell Charlotte had delivered them all: 12 little pink piggly wigglies, all of which were alive, healthy, and slurping away noisily with satisfying little grunts and squeals. Fortunately, Charlotte had 12 little faucets; one for each piglet.

By then it was 4 in the morning and it was too early for a cold Rainier Beer so I accepted some hot chocolate and an Oreo cookie instead. I pretended to hand out 12 cigars. After handshakes of congratulation and smiles of appreciation I headed home for a quick shower and what amounted to a short nap before the day's work began.

A month down the road, the Webbs had questions about iron injections and vaccinations for their growing swine herd. I was escorted back into the part of the garage which had been converted into Charlotte's private nursery until they could be turned outside when the weather warmed. The family car was still parked forlornly outside. Everywhere you looked there were wiggling bouncing squealing grunting little baby pigs. Charlotte appeared to be hiding off in a corner trying to avoid the assault of 12 hungry little snouts. Mr. Webb said, "I guess it's appropriate to introduce you to our rapidly increasing family." I noticed that they had apparently taken a pink permanent marker and put numbers on each piglet's back perhaps so they could identify and provide individualized care for each one. He said, "This is Fred 1, this is Fred 2, this is Fred 3," and so on and so on until he said, "And this is Fred 12. You were the only one who would come out to assist Charlotte in her moment of distress and we thought it appropriate that the babies be named in your honor. By the way, you have also been designated their godfather. Do you want to come to the christening? We are not, however, willing to offer up one of them in trade for the cost of services rendered."

I think that most of those piglets went on to become projects for the next county fair. I think the Webbs decided, after minimal reflection, to opt out of the swine business. I don't know if the precedent they set of saving a pig from market continued, but I strongly suspect that one of Charlotte's descendants is still out there producing the next batch of 4H projects.

GRADUATION PRESENT

Francine had always studied and worked hard, so the carrot held out in front by her parents had not been a necessary incentive. Mom and Dad had promised that if she did her share around the house and made the honor roll during her senior year, she would get the present that she had dreamed about even before she was old enough to drive: a pickup truck and horse trailer. Outside of her family, her horse was the most important thing in her life. Fancy was the first thing she thought about in the morning and the last thing she thought about at night. This put a lot of pressure on her parents because they spent much of their free time hauling Francine and her horse to shows and rodeo events. I'm sure they knew that it was a worthwhile trade off keeping her out of trouble and away from the reach of boys.

Friday night was graduation and Francine's name was on the graduation program for having been on the honor roll all through her high school years. Friday night was the graduation party and Francine and her friends stayed up late to celebrate. She woke up with a start late Saturday morning realizing that she had slept in and not gotten her morning chores done. She jumped out of bed, pulled on jeans and a sweatshirt, and ran out to the kitchen to apologize to her mom. "I'm sorry Mom. I forgot to set my alarm. I'll run right outside now and get my chores done."

Her mother said. "That's okay Francine. Dad and I took care of it. We knew you would be tired from the party last night. You might want to go out to the barn and make sure we did everything right." Francine open the door and looked out across the driveway towards the barn but there parked in the driveway was a pickup truck and a horse trailer. There was a note under the windshield wiper. Francine ran out and read the note which said, "Congratulations on your graduation Francine. Here is the promised present for a job well done. Love, Mom and Dad.".

Her dad came out and explained that, "The truck is a little old and has quite a few miles but I checked everything over and I know that it's safe and dependable. The trailer isn't all that fancy but it's certainly good enough for hauling your horse around the state."

Francine couldn't wait to try out her new truck and trailer and as soon as she ate breakfast and completed the few chores her mother hadn't already done, she loaded her horses to go out on a conditioning ride in the foothills north of town. She carefully backed out of the driveway and pulled out onto the road in front of their house and drove a few blocks down to the stop sign at the county road. She turned left and felt a sudden ominous lurching from behind. Disaster! Later examination would reveal two serious mistakes. The first mistake was that Dad had put a ball on the trailer hitch a size too small for the trailer. The second was that Francine was so eager to get underway that she neglected to attach the safety chains. When she turned the corner onto the county road the trailer hitch bounced off the ball and with no chain secure it to the truck, it rolled forward like a runaway hay wagon and tipped over into the deep county ditch. That's when I got the frantic telephone call. Fortunately, I had just finished up my mornings surgeries and my office was only about half a mile from the accident scene. I got there to see that the trailer was tipped in the ditch almost over on its roof. Francine and her father and brother we're desperately trying to calm the two struggling horses inside the trailer. They were almost on their backs like a turtle tipped upside down. The horses didn't not appear to have serious injury but that could soon change if they continued the violent struggling. With eight legs flying around there didn't appear to be any safe way to get the horses out of their predicament. There wasn't any time to come up with elaborate plan so I had to rely on my instincts. Kicking out a plastic window in the front of the trailer gave access to the horse's heads and necks. While standing in 3 feet of water I was lucky enough to get a substantial dose of anesthetic into their jugular veins. This left them unconscious but left us with 2400lb of dead weight. It did at least prevent them from doing further injury to themselves. Fortunately, by then, many people had stopped to help among which were some young strong farm boys who were Francine's classmates. We managed to get the back of the trailer open and using all the available manpower, grabbed hindlegs and tails and managed to pull the two horses out the back of the trailer. However, we were now trying to keep them afloat in three feet of water. I may have accidentally discovered the techniques that is sometimes now used in veterinary horse surgery recovery suites. When surgical repairs are made to horse's leg bones, one of the important hurdles to get past, is to get the horse back on its feet without undoing everything accomplished during the orthopedic surgery. One of the techniques that is sometimes now used is to recover the horse in water so that buoyancy allows the horse to gradually bear weight without going through the dramatic powerful struggling to get on its feet. This is what we had to do with Francine's two horses but we didn't have a modern water tank with flotation devices to help keep the horse from sinking. All we had were strong young men who stood there in the cold water trying to keep the horse's head afloat above water and avoiding flailing feet. Amazingly, after half an hour the horses were standing and alert enough that we could lead them down the ditch to a place where the bank was gradual enough to lead them up out of the water. The horses had a few scrapes and bumps and looked a little worse for wear and miraculously appeared to have no serious injuries. Dad came back with the tractor to right the trailer and pull it up out of the ditch. It had grass and mud all over one side but also amazingly, it too was not that much the worse for wear. Dad and her brother Jim were pretty sure that they could fix it up at home and put it back almost in the shape it had been in only an hour before.

Perhaps the most remarkable thing was that no one did any finger pointing or name blaming and everyone remarked, "What a blessing that there was no serious damage to the animals or equipment." A summer of fun and horsemanship had officially begun.

THE RANCHER AND HIS DOG

Frank had never married. A few cowgirls had shown some fleeting interest, perhaps hoping that it might be a little bit of silver underneath all that tarnish. They perhaps had also been inspired by the rumor, based on observations of Frank's frugality, that there might be some real silver and that old safe in the corner of Frank's living room. You could tell when there was some activity in Frank's relationship with the ladies because when he came into the clinic he would be recently shaved, have a new shirt, and even had freshly laundered Levi's on. The unlikely smell of cologne might also be evident. His footwear however, resisted all efforts towards upgrading and left their trademark signature of mud thoroughly mixed with cow manure on the reception room floor.

Frank was a talker; a slow, quiet, very long-winded talker. He was never too busy for a good conversation. It didn't seem to matter how busy you were or where you had to be, Frank always had something he wanted to say. You learned over time to always have ready-made excuse about where you needed to be. You didn't want to be rude but sometimes you required an escape plan if you didn't have an afternoon to *chew the fat.* He had two favorite sayings: "Thanks a million; until you're better paid," and "I made a mistake once. I thought I was wrong and I admitted it." I never could come up with an appropriate reply.

As Frank grew older, you could sense that he had given up on ever finding a lifetime companion. The evidence was overwhelming. There were the formerly white, but now permanently stained, shirts with strategic buttons missing, and Levi's that could probably stand unassisted in a corner when he took them off at night. His lawn had been unmowed for years and you had to hope that when his neighbors burned their ditches in the spring, they kept the fire away from his property for if his lawn ever caught fire it would take his unpainted tired old house with it. His barnyard had a mountain of hay wire accumulated overs 30 to 40 years. If his equipment ever broke down, chances are it was left parked where it had died with grass and even trees growing up around it or up through the floorboards.

There was one lady in his life however. She had the place of honor in his house, always got the choices parts of steak, and rode up beside him in his pickup truck. Her name was Sadie, also known as that *Naughty Lady*, and she was a crossbred Border Collie. There's something about the hair coat of a border collie that seems to be self-cleaning. In spite of where she lived and what she did Sadie always seem to be sparkling black and white.

69

People sometimes wondered to themselves if Sadie got more baths than Frank because she always had her best clean clothes on.

It was late hot summer afternoon when Frank called. Since my day's work was done, I settled down into the easy chair of my office anticipating a long conversation with Frank. He said, "I wuz out working cows on some of my leased rangeland and I plum forgot to bring any water for Sadie. I poured her a little bit of my beer in my hat but she kind of wrinkled her nose up at that. I wuz headed back t'home when I happened to look at my odometer and realized it'd been almost 30,000 miles since my last oil change. I thought, well, I'll just drive into that quick lube place and get it done before they shut 'er down this afternoon. Sadie wuz riding in the back of the pickup truck since it was cooler there and the AC crapped out about 5 years ago. I got out of my truck when I got there and went outside to roll a smoke. Sadie's never more'n about 10 feet from my heel so she, of course, followed me. I looked back to see her slurping something from a 5-gallon bucket. I asked the kid, Is that water?"

"He stared at me and said, 'Uh-oh! That's a bucket of antifreeze. I don't think dogs are supposed to drink it. Maybe you better call your vet and see if it's okay.' And so here I am."

All of a sudden, I realized that this was not a good time to have a long conversation with Frank. I asked him, "Where are you?"

He said, "I'm out on the other end of town at that quick lube joint."

I said "I want you to bring Sadie in right away. Now! And I want you to stop at the liquor store and get a pint of the strongest vodka that they sell."

He said, "What? Why?"

I said, "Frank! Just do it! Get here as quick as you can. I'll explain later." It turns out that ethylene glycol or antifreeze is a deadly poison for dogs as it destroys their kidneys. There's a liver enzyme called alcohol dehydrogenase that converts antifreeze to an oxalate. Oxalate crystals gets filtered out in the kidneys and cause major destruction. If you can get these dogs in quickly enough and start treatment you can save the kidneys. If you can bind all the alcohol dehydrogenase with alcohol, there is not enough left to form the oxalate crystals. 100% alcohol or ethanol, is hard to get, so if time is of the essence, we use high proof vodka.

Thus, my plan for Sadie was to establish an IV line and administer a slow vodka drip to the point where she was totally drunk. I explained all this to Frank. He quickly understood what I had in mind and asked, "How much will she need?"

I said, "I'm sure a pint will be enough but there's really no set dosage."

He said, "I'll grab two. That way there will be enough to share all around."

Shortly after, we heard his diesel truck growl to a stop at the front door. We needed to establish an IV line and carefully drip vodka in and observe her level of inebriation.

Frank said, "I got nothing better to do this evening so can I flop here to keep her company?"

I said, "Sure. We can pull up a chair alongside the kennel and you can be comfortable there." We shaved the hair off over the vein on Sadie's right front leg, scrubbed it, and inserted an intravenous indwelling catheter. It didn't take long to get the IV drip going and have Sadie comfortably relocated to one of our large kennels on a pile of dog blankets.

Frank said, "Gimme a minute, I'm gunna go outside to roll a homemade and then I'll be right back." About 10 minutes later Frank came back and established himself comfortably in the chair alongside Sadie's kennel. After a minute or two you sense he was uncomfortable and then he stood up and removed the second pint vodka from his hip pocket. This made us remember one of Franks other notorious habits. He did like his liquor.

Later that evening after we had finished Sadie's treatment, I called the local cab company. I informed the dispatcher that I had two passengers that needed to be delivered to their home northeast of town. He asked, "What's the address and what are their names?"

I said, "They're here at my veterinary hospital and their names are Frank and Sadie. By the way they're both staggering drunk and it might be a challenge getting them into their house. I'll cover the taxi fair." We called Frank the next day and after making sure he was in shape to drive ask him to bring Sadie in for some continuing blood tests. They came in late in the day both bedraggled, red-eyed, and looking pretty hungover. We checked Sadie's blood and urine and both fell within normal range so we had dodged a medical bullet in terms of Sadie's health.

Frank said, "It shore is great to share a bottle with your best friend, but the doctoring wuz pretty hard on both of us so I think we'll pack it in for the rest of the of the week to recover."

LUCKY

After my father retired as a chemistry professor, my parents spent the summer months at Campbell River on Vancouver Island. My father had remodeled a single wide mobile home which was located on a gravely spit where the river enters Discovery Passage. It was a great place for a change of pace for my family and for me from the busy daily routine as a veterinarian. You could sit on their deck all day just watching the fishing boats, cruise ships, tug boats, recreational boaters, and seaplanes as they passed through the narrowing waters of Discovery Passage. Occasionally a local pod of Orca would pause to clean out all the chinook salmon from the famous Tyee Salmon Pool. They could be seen working the pool only 100 feet from the shore. Fishing there would be pointless for the following week

74

We sometimes ran our small cabin cruiser up from Horseshoe Bay near Vancouver through the Salish Sea to Campbell River. We had purchased the boat used but decided that a veterinarian's boat needed an appropriate name so on the starboard bow we stenciled Push Me and, on the port bow we stenciled Pull U. You may recall that Dr. Doolittle had a double headed llama that he called a pushmipullu. (The original book had a gazelle head on one end and a unicorn head on the other. The advantage to the animal was that it could eat and talk at the same time. I'm not sure how it took care of other body functions),

Campbell River was a fantastic area for doing anything outdoors on the water. Fishing for Chinook and Coho salmon was great. I was once lucky enough to catch a 63lb chinook salmon. Bottom fish such as rock cod and lingcod were plentiful and at any low tide it was easy to find all varieties of clams and Olympic oysters. A crab pot provided hor d'oeuvres

During that period, Campbell River was supposed to be the busiest seaplane port in the world. In the morning there was a constant drone of sea planes taking off to deliver loggers and supplies up the British Columbia coast to floating logging camps and fishing resorts. Aviation rules were rather lax and so occasionally we would sign on at cargo rates to go along on these fights. The trade-off was that we were then the dock hands to help secure the float plane to the docks and to unload the cargo being delivered. It was always exciting on the initial take off to see if the overloaded Beaver seaplane would ever get airborne. It lumbered and grumbled and growled and bounced and skipped. If you gave a nervous glance to the pilot he just looked over and smiled. I guess he figured he was in no hurry to die that day either.

The Campbell River Resort was mainly occupied during the summer months by people who love fishing and saltwater activities. It had its own private dock situated in freshwater just up the river a short distance. In the evening there was usually a gathering of many of the people from the resort at the dock to greet the incoming fleet. The fleet amounted to the people who had been out sports fishing during the day and were returning with whatever they had caught.

One day there was an unusually large crowd at the dock and I wandered over to see what the excitement was. I heard Mrs. Martin say, "You'll never believe what we caught today. It only weighed about 15 lbs. but it sure put up a struggle." Just then her husband John came out from the boat cabin and in his arms, he held a small black and brown Boston Terrier. I listened in as the story was eventually revealed. The Martins and some friends had traveled from Campbell River about 20 miles to the east to a place known as Marina Island. It was famous because that at a good low tide, the cockles were especially plentiful. They are a clam that could actually be found just lying on the surface or only barely covered in the sand. So, gathering them was especially easy. They rowed ashore in their dinghy and rather quickly gathered several buckets of the heavily ribbed clam and then had a picnic sitting on beach driftwood while waiting for the tide to return and refloat their dinghy. After returning to the big boat, they washed up and relaxed at anchor for a while to have a Molson beer and talk about the pleasant day they had enjoyed. Eventually, they hauled anchor and headed back across the Malaspina Strait towards Campbell River. About halfway back, perhaps 10 miles from the nearest land, they noticed something off the starboard bow splashing in the water. They continued on but eventually their curiosity got the better of them and they circled back.

As they motored closer, they discovered that it was a small brown dog. John suggested to his wife, "Martha, why don't you get the salmon net out and we'll see if we can catch it." Obviously, the poor thing had seen the boat approaching and it was paddling desperately. Martha expertly scooped him up in the net and lifted him aboard. It lay there on the deck for several minutes just shivering and gasping heavily. Martha went below and got a towel and sat on the floorboards beside the poor little guy and dried him off. Eventually he sat up, looked around to get his bearings, and with a big sigh, crawled over into her lap and began licking her hands.

Eventually she picked him up and carried him over to their most comfortable cabin chair and sat with him in her lap wrapped up in a blanket. She said once they got underway again, he fell asleep and slept in her lap all the way back to Campbell River.

Everybody knew that I was a veterinarian so they called me over to examine a little dog. Amazingly, he appeared not much the worse for wear. Its teeth indicated that he was only two or three years old. His toenails have been recently clipped so someone must have been taking care of him. And then of course the inevitable questions began. Where did he come from? How did he get there? Who does he belong to?

We could only assume that he had fallen off of somebody's boat and his disappearance had been unnoticed. You can only imagine the thoughts going through the little guy's head as he watched his cruise ship sailing off into the sunset without him. Did they come back looking for him? Who knows? I suggested that they talk to local law enforcement RCMP, animal shelters, veterinary offices, and even post notices at local marinas. A few days later my vacation time was up and I had to get on my own boat and head towards Vancouver and eventually home. The Martins were good friends with my parents and I exchanged telephone numbers and addresses with them so they could keep me posted. I forgot all about that little brown and black Boston

Terrier until about three months later in October when I got a long letter from the Palm Springs area of Southern California. Martha wrote me detailing everything else that happened. They had advertised every way that they could think of while providing a safe controlled environment and loving care for the dog. The guests at the resort often gathered around a bonfire in the evening and about a week later there was discussion as to what his name might be.

Someone piped up. "Obviously his name is Lucky. How else could he have been found in thousands of square miles of open water by a boat that just happened to be passing within sight". They kept him and loved him hoping that somehow his true owners could be located. They never were. Come October, it was time to leave the fishing haven of British Columbia and travel south for the winter. Martha said that Lucky was a much-loved member of their family in spite of his Canadian accent and he was enjoying the warm sunny days of the Southern California winter. He didn't seem too fond of fish or seafood but actually could sometimes be seen in their backyard eating kumquats that fell from their tree. Unbelievably, when the weather got hot, he would jump in and swim in their outdoor pool to cool off. They said he had a very impressive dog paddle. We saw Lucky a few times in the succeeding years. He was, of course, a permanent member of the Martin family and traveled back and forth as a snow bird in the spring and fall between Palm Springs and Campbell River. When I would visit them in their travel trailer or sit on their deck, inevitably Lucky would jump up into my lap and lick my face. You might assume that he was eternally happy with everybody because of his good fortune of having been rescued at sea.

GUNNER

Mel's life never lacked for variety. He really had two advocations and said, "It's hard to say which one I love most. I could never decide between being a cowboy or a sailor." He liked working on old wooden boats. It required old school woodworking skills to repair old damaged wooden parts and also the skill and knowledge to replace caulking. His other love was cattle and he had a small cattle ranch in the eastern foothills of the Cascades. When he was working on a boat near salt water, he could be a live aboard tenant wearing his old seaman's cap and stay on whatever craft he was repairing. Otherwise he was at home playing cowboy wearing his battered sweat stained Stetson.

Getting to his ranch was almost like an exploration road trip. You drove past the irrigated hay fields and then over a canal that brought snowmelt water from mountain reservoirs. A gravel road led up through sagebrush into a small canyon where a gurgling stream flowed past cottonwoods and willows that lined the bank.

79

You passed pole corrals before you saw the old log ranch house tucked in amongst a grove of ponderosa pines. There was a backdrop of basalt columns that stood like guardians behind the house. You needed a good 4WD truck to get there in the winter. If you stopped inside by the wood burning stove it could be hard to pry yourself away as well.

To be a cattleman, first of all you have to have a ranch. The money he earned working on boats enabled him to post a large down payment on the property. That accomplished the first requirement. Then you have to have cows. One way to achieve this is to go to cattle sales and buy old cows that more prosperous cattlemen were culling from their herds. These animals are usually cheap and if well-cared for, can usually deliver several more babies until they again return to the sales barn. Then you have to have horses. When you get to know local cattlemen, you find they sometimes have old horses that are still useful but not quite up to the task of working cattle all day long. Such horses can be bought pretty cheap if you assure the former owner that the workload will be light and the horse will be well cared for. And finally, you have to have a cattle dog. Around these parts the healer is the breed most frequently seen.

The proper name for the breed is the Australian Cattle Dog which is sometimes known down under as just the Cattle Dog. Around here we typically refer to them as Blue Heelers or Red Heelers depending on whether they have black hair or brown hair interspersed amongst the basically white coat. This is called ticking and there is a gene in their DNA for this kind of hair coat. They are a muscular sturdy breed averaging about 45lb and 18 inches at the shoulder. They have erect alert ears and are born with a naturally long tail which acts like a rudder when they are working cattle. They could be called a self-cleaning appliance, for if they get muddy, they soon dry off and slick out and look as clean and bright as ever. They tend to shed their coat out once a year unlike Border Collies who shed continually.

Descriptive terms include: solid, active, durable, hard headed, independent, one person, intelligent, protective, and with a natural instinct to bite at the heels of livestock in an effort to herd them.

Mel had such a dog and his name was Gunner. He either rode shotgun in the cab of the pickup or stood guard just behind the driver seat in the truck box. When he was working on boats Gunner was the night watchman and the lookout responsible for patrolling the deck. He could work tirelessly all day on cattle in the corral or cover great distances when Mel was out on the range checking the cattle grazing out in the sagebrush. He could get distracted by ground squirrels or other ground-dwelling small mammals but usually could be called back to the task at hand when chastised by the boss. Mel said, "I love my wife but Gunner doesn't talk back when we work the cows."

One of the drawbacks to livestock dogs is that they need work. If you don't give them a task, they often find one for themselves. This could include excavating vole tunnels. chasing ground squirrels, and running long distances after birds even after they were airborne. Unfortunately, not all the animals he pursued were totally harmless. When he got sprayed by a skunk, he had to reside in the outdoor bachelor quarters., hopefully downwind, until the odor disappeared. When he jumped in the water trough or a stream to cool down, it was evident who his previous playmate had been.

Sadly, the other animal he relentlessly pursued was the porcupine. The porcupines seem to come down to lower pasture elevations in the spring and fall to feed on the inner layers of bark on willows and cottonwoods when the sap was running, and

81

Gunner was always ready. Mel was there when Gunner encountered his first porcupine. He initially approached this strange animal cautiously not knowing quite what to make of it. But when he got to close, the porcupine slapped him in his face with its quill studded tail. Porcupine quills are fascinating because when they are driven into something, a special mechanism allows them to be released from their owner's body. Otherwise, a porcupine accidentally bumping into a fence post would be stuck there *till death do us part*. Once Gunner got a face full of porcupine quills Mel said, "He became enraged and attacked with a vengeance." Each attempt to get at the porcupine only increased his misery and Mel said the only way he could separate them was to grab him by his convenient tail and drag him out of harm's way. "The porcupine was unharmed and just waddled off." I was a little dismayed to see him on this occasion. His looked like he had a full beard made of porcupine quills. Remarkably, dog's eyes never seen to be injured in these events for there is a muscle that can retract the eye back into the socket thus sparing it from being stabbed. We carefully got Gunner up on the table not wanting to hug him too closely. We knew it was going to take some time to get all the quills out so I gave him a short acting dose of anesthetic and then put him on the anesthesia machine to achieve inhaled volatile gas anesthesia. Mel, myself, and my veterinary assistant each grabbed a pair of forceps and began pulling.

There is no easy way. Cutting them in half makes no difference. They just are a hard durable needle sharp weapon that has microscopic barbs on the tip. With one hand you support the skin around the quill and with the other hand you pull until the quill comes out. We worked for about an hour and lost count the number of quills. There had to been seven or eight hundred of them all together. Inevitably, some break off or are not discovered in spite of your best efforts at quill braille. We usually

82

have these dogs come back in three to five days where we again feel all over their bodies to find those that we missed on the on the first attempt. When Gunner came back for his recheck, he seemed none the worse for wear and was his usual self-confident self. Mel and I talked about cattle prices, the quality of spring range grass, and how he needed to get a replacement bull that spring. We shook hands and they disappeared out the front door to load into the truck for the drive back to the ranch.

Three days later Mel and Gunner were back; same story only not quite as many quills at this time. Perhaps that porky had donated too many quills the first time and had yet to regrow them. Seven days later they were back again. It didn't take a mind-reader to sense that Mel was getting a little frustrated with the determined but questionable behavior of his cattle dog. We discussed the habits of porcupines and I said, "I suspect the porcupine is not too far away from the house and you're going to have to go out and locate him or Gunner will just keep going after him. I'm not sure if a dog could kill a porcupine. They're actually surprisingly agile and tough."

Next time I saw Mel it was late in the fall and we were vaccinating some of his calves. Gunner was there helping to move the cattle down the runway into the shoot. I said, "He doesn't look that much the worst for were considering what he went through this spring." Mel said, "After that third quill pulling exercise, I knew I had to find and eliminate Mr. Porcupine. The next day when Gunner had recovered, I saddled up old Rusty and the three of us went out on a porcupine safari. I thought he might be up in the creek bottom back up behind the ranch house so we headed out that way once morning chores were done. I've never seen a bird dog work but I guess now I can say I seen a porcupine dog work. He cast around and quickly picked up a trail and trotted off determinedly up the canyon.

Rusty and I rode hard to keep up and be close where I could watch Gunner but he was so determined that he ignored my shouts and seemed to know exactly where he was going. I thought to myself, "Uh oh! Here we go again." The terrain got rough so Rusty and I lost sight of Gunner. When we finally found him, he was frantically running around and barking at the base of a small white fir tree looking up at Mr. Porcupine who was calmly perched about 15 feet off the ground. You could see where he had been chewing on the inner layers of bark. 'Boy, are we ever lucky that the porcupine was not on the ground,' I said to Gunner, 'I think when we're done with this we need to go into town to the casino and do some gambling because our luck is running really strong today.' I tied Gunner to a small tree a safe distance away with baling twine and reluctantly but determinedly got out my 38 to eliminate our problem once and for all. When the job was done, I found a large rock I was just barely able to tip over. Using a stick, I excavated an appropriate size hole underneath it and cautiously deposited Mr. Porcupine in his permanent resting place. After replacing the dirt, I tipped the rock back over and sat on it and said a final silent 'Amen! I'm sure glad that's over.' I wanted to secure Mr. Porcupine in such a way that there was no risk to Gunner or other animals and I certainly wasn't about to carry him in the saddle with me back to the ranch."

But this is not the end of the story. I saw Gunner a few times more when he had an especially large face full. Mel had become moderately proficient in relatively painless porcupine quill extraction. Gunner knew he had messed up and sat patiently with occasional quiet growls and yelps while Mel pulled a few porcupine quills. Each time there were less quills so Gunner was either luckier or was slowly learning to be more careful.

About 10 years later Mel came in one Saturday morning and said, "The owners of the last boat I worked on just had a litter of Blue Heeler puppies. I decided to take one as partial payment for my work. We lost Gunner last fall. One morning he just didn't show up for work and we found him in permanent peaceful sleep in his bed of straw in the barn. My wife and the kids and I sat down that day when we discovered that Gunner had departed and tried to make a count of the porcupine quill extraction episodes. As best we could tell, Gunner had encountered porcupines 23 times. We had to dispatch about half a dozen of them and wondered if they were all related and had a life mission to harass Gunner. We also jokingly considered getting an affidavit regarding these 23 episodes to send into the Guinness Book of World Records to see if Gunner was a world record porcupine hunter. He's resting out at the base of those columns behind the house."

"And now, I'd like you to meet Gunner II."

TREASURE HUNT

Joan and Frank were Dachshund owners. They were a special breed: the Doxie Owners breed that is. Well, the dachshunds are a special breed too. Most dog owners like to brag about their pets a little bit. They talk about how quiet they are, how easy they are to train, how respectful they are to their owners, how polite they are around the food dish, and how they never beg. Doxie owners, however, brag about how independent their pets are, how they gobble down and compete for food, how they sometimes even come when called, and how they resist almost all attempts at training. When pressed, they would probably reluctantly admit that the Doxies were the owners and the people were the pets. Yes! Joan and Frank were classic Doxie owners.

We used to tease Joan and Frank that they had met at a canine obedience class after their dogs had either been expelled or failed the final exam (walking on a leash). After they married and combined their families, they had a small herd of five dachshunds: Heidi, Heather, Hanna, Hailey, and Holly. They jokingly said that they would have more except they ran out of "*H*" names from the alphabet. A doorbell was unnecessary because even the quietest knock on the front door sent off five 90 decibel alarm systems. If you manage to get over the threshold, then there was an obstacle course of brown barking belligerent bouncing bodies and doggy toys in varying states of dismemberment or destruction.

Fortunately, they had a large house with many rooms. The dogs were so competitive at mealtime that a barking snarling biting contest could ensue. The only solution was to give each dog its own private dining room at meal time. Each of the "*H*" dogs got a half hour to finish its meal and then the food dishes were picked up. There was one benefit to this program for it did allow very careful weight control for the dogs.

Doxies are snugglers and burrowers, so after dinner when the family sat down in the living room to read or watch TV, there was generally a race to see who got to occupy the prime location next to his human servant. The result was that Joan usually had one dog on either side and one dog in her lap under the blanket while Frank had to settle for one dog on either side as he tried to find room for his own body in the Lazy Boy.

Was this instinctive doxie competitiveness the cause of Heidi's predicament? I guess we will never know because there were no witnesses and doxies, in spite of their high intelligence, have never learned to talk. If they could, I'm sure that somebody would have ratted out the guilty party

Joan said, "Frank! Have you seen my pantyhose?

He replied, "No! The last time I saw them they were on the floor in the bathroom where you took them off last night before your shower." Just then they heard that telltale urping sound of a dog attempting to vomit from the vicinity of the living room shag carpet. This is not an uncommon event due to the doxie's gluttonous dinner time habits. In the rush to clean up the mess on the carpet the mystery of the disappearing pantyhose remained unsolved. Heidi's appetite disappeared for the next 24 hours and the attempts at vomiting continued so Joan and Frank brought her in for an examination. Heidi didn't try to bite me so we knew something must be seriously amiss. Lab results were within the normal range so we decided an x-ray was appropriate. The film revealed an enlarged stomach with apparently some sort of the mass inside. It was therefore reluctantly decided that further exploration was appropriate. We gave her a short-acting anesthetic and passed a fiber optic endoscope through mouth, down the esophagus, and into her stomach. It was not possible to determine exactly what was there but it was some sort of a fibrous mass that was unlikely to pass on through or be retrievable with the endoscope. Consequently, we just continued and prepared Heidi for an exploratory surgery. About 20 minutes later we were making a very careful incision through the greater curvature of the stomach wall. After carefully packing off the area in case of spillage, we begin extracting the strange material. We gently emptied and emptied and emptied until finally everything was removed and we were able to admire the site of a still healthy and empty stomach cavity. Two careful rows of sutures closed the stomach wall. After the abdominal cavity was carefully flushed many times with sterile saline, the stomach was placed back in its favorite parking place and the body wall and skin were sutured.

John and Frank were from out of town so they had waited anxiously in a nearby motel to hear the outcome. We called them and were glad to report that Heidi had come through the procedure just fine and all her systems seemed normal. We expected a full and complete recovery.

You could hear the relief in their voice when they said, "That's certainly good news. Thank you so much."

Joan asked, "What did you find in her stomach?"

I said, "I don't know. We were so intent on taking care of Heidi that we haven't even looked. I guess we need to retrieve it from the garbage can."

They said, "We'll come right down so we can be there to comfort our baby as she wakes up." They sat in the recovery area with Heidi in their lap. We rummaged around among the various disgusting items in the garbage can to retrieve the mysterious item. We washed it off and displayed it to the worried parents. You guessed it. It was an intact pair of pantyhose. How did Heidi manage to swallow them down and do so a little damage? I told Joan, "They look almost as good as new. I suspect if you took them home and washed them, they would be ready to wear for your next ballroom dance."

This was not Heidi's first episode of dietary indiscretion but it was the first one requiring surgical intervention. At last report the doxie herd was in training to pull a sled (with wheels) for an upcoming doxie parade and competition. Such a team, if equipped with warm coats, could be invaluable in the winter time if there was a snowstorm of no more than 1 inch of snow.

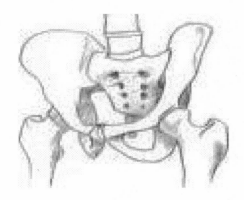

500 MILE RIDE

It was only going to be a three-day horse camping trip into the William O. Douglas Wilderness Area. However, it took five years to finally finish the ride. We loaded up the horses about 6 AM on a bright sunny Saturday morning in June. There were three riders: me, my wife, and her 13-year-old youngest daughter. We had four horses so rather than leave one home alone, we let our gelding Seuss tag along loose behind. He thought he was pretty special traveling along unattended. I didn't have a packsaddle at the time so with horn bags, saddlebags, and the sleeping bag tied on top, we left the trailhead up into the cool old growth timber of the Mesatchee Creek.

The day was warm but the tall trees kept it cool and pleasant as we followed the gently climbing trail. Some browsing deer watched us walk by, and the occasional grouse scented by our dog flew up to a branch and clucked at us we rode underneath.

There was one adrenaline-pumping moment as we managed to escape, unstung, from a stirred-up nest of ground hornets.

We were about three to four miles in when disaster struck. My horse was a tremendously muscled mare who was a direct descendant from a famous quarter horse named Poco Bueno from the King Ranch in Texas. She was an unusually sure-footed mountain horse and truly loved leading our rides along mountain trails. We were fording a branch of the American River when it happened. The ford was calm quiet clear water that was belly deep to a horse. You had to lift your boots up to keep them from filling with water. Unaccountably, my mare whirled and like a bucking hippo came lunging back to the original bank. I have no idea what spooked her or caused this explosion. If she had thrown me off in the process, I would have been cold and soaked and madder than a hooked catfish but I managed to stay on board actually being somewhat trapped by all the gear attached to the saddle. She flipped me up in the air and when gravity decided to let me come back down, she was lunging back up and I was hammered into the saddle.

I instantly knew that I had broken my pelvis. When she returned to dry ground, she stood quivering to collect herself. I remember saying, "I've broken my pelvis," but have no recollection of how my wife and stepdaughter were able to get me off the horse onto the ground. I lay there in shock in the dirt trying to manufacture an organized thought and decide what to do. Eventually, a little color returned to my face, the nauseous sensation waned, and my brain began to marginally function again. We realized that a helicopter was best but there was no place that we had seen to land and the heavy timber would have prevented dropping a basket from above. If we sent someone out for help how are you going to handle the logistics. Would my 13-year-old step-daughter stay with me and my wife go for help or vice versa? We were about an hour and a half ride from the trailhead. There was no cell service and the nearest land line was about 20 miles down towards Rimrock Lake. If someone went for help it would be perhaps five or six hours before a ground crew with a wheeled gurney could return.

The shock had subsided somewhat and it appeared I wasn't going to die so we decided we would attempt to get me back on a horse and do a self-rescue. This is where our fourth horse, Seuss, came into play. We often called such a ponied horse our spare tire. He was by far our gentlest horse but he did not like to be the lead horse. If he traveled in front, he slowed everybody else down. By piling smooth flat rocks in such a way as to make a staircase up alongside a large downed log and using shoulders for support and steadiness, I managed to stand on top of the log. Seuss stood there very patiently seeming to appreciate my predicament. They lowered me into the saddle in a side saddle fashion.

I have no recollection of how we got my leg over the saddle horn to where I sat astride his back. Initially, we tried having my step daughter lead him, but it proved to be almost impossible for my wife to handle the other three horses behind. Ultimately, I rode Seuss in front by myself and they rode and led the other horse behind. Seuss knew a few voice commands and we slowly proceeded down the trail. When my vision dimmed and I began to black out I would whisper, "Whoa" and he would stand there until I could again see before continuing on down the trail. We had shortened the stirrups as much as possible so that my legs could take some of the weight and if I leaned forward with my hands on the pommels of the saddle, we could travel on down the trail for a few hundred feet. I don't know how long it took to get to the trailhead but it was at least 10 years and covered well over 500 miles.

After an eternity, just as we got to the trailhead a big lifted four-wheel drive 250 Ford pickup pulled into the parking lot and three big burly guys jumped out looking for something to do with their excess testosterone. I unhappily provided just the challenge they needed. They got me out of the saddle, funneled into a sleeping bag, and enthroned shotgun style in the passenger seat of our truck. My wife had never driven the truck with the camper and four horses in the trailer behind, but she performed admirably and we got underway down highway 410. Even though I was in the sleeping bag I was still shivering.

When we got to Yakima, we had a brief discussion about whether to go to an emergency room there and I said, "We made it this far. We might just as well keep on going home to Ellensburg." So, an hour later we drove up to the emergency entrance at KVH with me, the pickup with a camper, and four horses in the horse trailer. We had dirt under our fingernails, dirty sweaty streaks down our faces, dirty muddy Levi's, and horse manure on our boots. But at least there was no blood and our deodorant was still working. An x-ray revealed that I had separated my pubic symphysis about one half inch.

Fortunately, my friend, an orthopedic surgeon, was there doing afternoon rounds on his patients. After a quick consultation, we agreed that right now was as good a time as any to screw me back together. The options were to fly me to Harborview in Seattle, take me back to Yakima to a doctor more experienced in pelvic injuries, or take care of me right here right now. By then, with some injected opioids, I was feeling no pain and jokingly said, "This is an injury I have repaired many times on dogs and cats. If I just had an appropriately placed rear view mirror, I could probably do the surgery myself. The doctor smiled, and a half an hour later I was counting backwards from 10 in the anesthesia induction room prior to going in for surgery.

It turns out that I had seriously damaged the belly muscles that attach to the pubic bone and the doctor and his assistant spent most of the time reattaching the muscles.

I went home the next day and luxuriated in family sympathy for a day or two but they ran out of sympathy. Also, I quickly became bored and thus decided to go back to work. I was able to perform almost everything at the office by sitting in a wheeled office chair and propelling myself backwards like a runaway bus with no rear-view mirrors. Muscle and soft tissue healed nicely but the bones were more reluctant. If I stood and rocked from left to right on my heels, I could feel the bones grind uncomfortably against each other. The medical term is crepitus. It was a strange sensation but not terribly painful so I decided to get on with my life and in about four months was even foolishly back on my horse. I guess it's kind of a *guy thing*.

However, the grating sensation continued and eventually another x-ray revealed that the screws in the plate holding my pelvis together had loosened and needed to be removed. I don't suppose the poor healing had anything to do with the fact that I continued my usual active lifestyle. So, it was done. But life is too short to sit around waiting for things to heal to perfection so I just got on with my usual routine. From time to time I would rock back on my heels and determined that the grinding sensation in my pelvis was still there. And this is where my story finally comes to an end.

Five years later in the month of June, I discovered that the crepitus was finally gone. My pelvis had finally healed and I was left only with a C-section type scar on my belly and a peculiar knot of scar tissue in my lower belly muscles. When horse people gather together, they sometimes like to swap lies about the injuries they have received from their prized harmless equine possessions. My favorite line under these circumstances is to

94

explain that I am one of the few men who has enjoyed all the pleasures of childbirth but never had anything to show for the effort. Perhaps I have more understanding of what my wife went through when she delivered our son. We both had the pleasure of raising him together and watching him grow to adulthood so she was well rewarded for her effort.

Later that summer we packed our camping gear and loaded the horses to finally complete the ride into the William O. Douglas Wilderness that we began five years earlier. I didn't get bucked off that time.

BUD - WISER

Every morning began as a huge disappointment for Bud, but every day ended with a moment of great joy and happiness. The Boss was a school bus driver who drove the bus home every night after finishing her route. They lived in a tidy little house with a wrap-around porch. It was up near the end of the pavement in a beautiful timbered valley with interspaced hay fields in the meadows. Every morning Bud was told to stay when The Boss climbed the steps up to the driver seat of the bus. You could see the hopeful happy expression just melt off of his face and his happily wagging tail droop to half-mast. He dejectedly ambled back down the lane, up the steps, and onto the porch where he was destined to stay guarding the house until the end of the day. He watched the birds fly overhead, scented an occasional deer grazing out in the meadow, and observed the postie deliver mail to the box at the end of the lane.

And then joy of joys, at a time that his internal clock exactly predicted, the yellow bus appeared off in the distance, slowed, and turned down the lane to expire in the barnyard with a cough. The door clattered open and his joy and excitement knew no bounds. The Boss was home. He had not been forgotten and was about to be rewarded with her unending love for faithfully doing his job all day long. As a bonus for his diligence he was often rewarded with half-eaten sandwiches, remnants from snack packs of chips, pickles, and whatever other edible items that had been left on the bus by the untidy children. Bud was a large yellow Labrador, so his gut was made of cast iron and managed to survive these daily disturbances.

One Friday a child left a small rubber ball on the bus. The Boss had heard it thump and rattle around from side to side and forward and back as the bus stopped, accelerated, or made turns. It took a while to find it there behind the wheel well on the right-hand side. The Boss picked it up and carried it forward without thinking. She said to herself, "I bet Bud would like to play with this," and tossed it into the air. He saw it coming and with perfect timing, leaped up into the air to catch it but somehow in his eagerness he caught it with his mouth open too wide and ***down the hatch*** it went. To his surprise he realized he had just swallowed a small red Super Ball. The Boss didn't even know what had happened and finished sweeping out the bus and went into the house to change into her barn clothes so she could finish the chores of feeding the chickens and ducks and check on the cow and horses.

The next day something with seemed a little amiss with Bud. He wasn't really sick but had lost his appetite and seemed a little lethargic. He still helped with the chores and followed The Boss around all day doing weekend farm chores. Sunday he was worse. His belly rumbled noisily; you could hear it all the way across the room. He could keep water down but was often outside eating grass and trying to retch it back up. The Boss called us Monday morning for an appointment. "I'll bring him down as soon as I finish my bus route," she said. At 4:30 pm they arrived in the parking lot and Bud weakly followed The Boss through the door. He gave a weak wag of his tail in recognition and lay quietly down on the cool floor. No one yet knew what the problem could be so we played VCSI (veterinary crime scene investigator) asking questions that might help make a diagnosis. He was now severely dehydrated so we started an IV line and then took an X-Ray. The fluid and gas build up in part of the intestine indicated some sort of a blockage. The three day *wait and see* had accomplished nothing so we prepped him for exploratory surgery. He gave a relaxing audible sigh and a loud belch when the sedative took effect. In no time we had him opened up wide with all his insides on full display. Little by little we eased the intestinal tract out on the sterile surgical drape to examine every inch of its entire length. Then we found an enlarged angry dark red section of intestine which had to be the blockage. Everything was returned to its usual place leaving the jeopardized section outside where it could be isolated to prevent leakage and contamination when it was opened. A small incision in the ileum (first part of the small intestine) revealed a small red rubber ball which slowly rolled off the drape, onto the surgery table, and then bounced merrily across the surgery room floor. That small section of intestine was too damaged to survive so we removed it and then sewed the healthy remaining ends back together (called an anastomosis). Copious amounts of warm sterile saline were used to flush the repaired section and all was returned to reside happily in its usual and accustomed place. We called The Boss to report that Bud was doing well and explain what we had found. Then she remembered what had happened. She said, "I wondered what Bud and done with that little red rubber ball and he was hiding it the whole time." Bud went home the next day to be gradually returned to a full ration of soft food. The speed and effectiveness of healing in the canine intestine is truly amazing. Dogs start eating the next day and, in fact, do better than if they are held off food for a few days. The Boss, to the delight of the children, brought Bud along with her on the bus the next week so she could keep an eye on him. The kids were cautioned that, "He is allowed no treats." Things quickly returned to normal and The Boss watched carefully to see that nothing but food found its way down Bud's throat. Summer arrived and the bus was parked at the school garage until Fall. The Boss was home all day where Bud could watch and help her with all the farm chores and events. We decided to amend Bud's birth certificate so that his name would now be Budwiser, having learned his lesson the hard way .

CANADIAN ADVENTURE

The plan had always been to get my DVM degree and then join a practice in the town where I grew up. During my senior year of vet school, they modified the curriculum and there was a one-time opportunity to take advanced clinical courses. One such course was advanced small animal surgery. Usually two students paired up alternating as surgeon and assistant. At the last moment, my partner found he had been offered a job as the Assistant State Veterinarian for the state of Nevada. That left me without a surgery partner which was a blessing in disguise. I had the opportunity to do two practice surgeries each week but without an assistant. You learn quickly and prepare very carefully when everything rests on your own shoulders.

When the time came for me to graduate and join the expected local practice, there had been an economic downturn and another veterinarian was not needed. So, the plan changed and I would work elsewhere for a year, gain valuable experience, and then return when economic conditions were better. Since it was only going to be for a year, my wife and I decided we may as well go someplace unique and there was an opportunity to join a practice in Nanaimo on Vancouver Island. When I interviewed, they asked me what my salary expectations were. I had done my homework and realized the Canadian veterinarians were better paid and that you also had to consider the rate of exchange of US dollars. I was offered the job on my terms and we shook hands on it. I went back home to complete my studies and waited for a confirmation phone call from them.

The call never came. Finally, I called for an explanation. They said that one of my classmates had been willing to do the job for considerably less. He asked to be paid the same that he would have been in the States but did not realize that Canadian veterinarians made more money and that Canadian dollars were worth less. Of course, they said he could have the job but they never got around to telling me that I had been under bid.

Another opportunity occurred in the town of Mission which was only about 20 miles across the Canadian border. I interviewed there with Dr. Paddy and we got along well so that when he offered me a job I accepted. Only 3 months later he asked me if I wanted to buy into the practice and become an equal partner. His previous partner had retired and sold his half of the practice to Paddy who had gone through a number of disastrous associates.

Paddy was of German descent and was desperate to get some time away to visit his father who still lived in Berlin, Germany. My advanced classes and exposure to the latest techniques and diagnostic equipment made me an asset to his practice. I had only been there four months when he asked me if I thought I was ready to go solo. He said, "I haven't seen my Grossvater for 6 years and he is in failing health. I have to go see him while I still can".

So, only six months out of school suddenly, I am the ***doctor in charge***. I certainly grew to appreciate the rigorous training I received at the WSU College of Veterinary Medicine but I also spent long midnight hours in the books trying to be prepared for scheduled procedures the next day. The work day of a veterinarian is often full of surprises and one can only hope that your training prepared you to handle them. For many of those events there is no way to study the night before.

Our practice had an unusual work schedule. Essentially, you worked 10 days sometimes with your partner and sometimes without and then had four days off. Those four days off were almost mini-vacations. We purchased a small cabin cruiser and spent wonderful days on what is called the Salish Sea. I also became a member of the Ski Patrol and due to my irregular work schedule, was able to choose the hours for ski patrolling and surprisingly, those hours usually coincided with the days following a heavy snowfall. Camping, fishing, and exploring filled the rest of our free time.

We loved those years in British Columbia but when it was time for our son to start school, we had some tough decisions to make. In that community high school dropout rates could reach 35%. Smoking was common among teenagers and of those who finished high school only 3% to 4% went on to university. We decided this was not the educational environment in which we wanted to raise our son, so after six years the time finally came to return to Ellensburg to join the practice that I had planned on so many years before.

We were back in Ellensburg signing papers to purchase a house east of town on the day when Mount St Helens erupted. When it turned totally dark in the middle of the day due to falling ash, the pastures of Canada were looking pretty green. I have lived in Kittitas County, Washington State, ever since.

A FULL BUS LOAD

Jed just managed to graduate from high school but probably wouldn't have bothered if his parents hadn't insisted. He was the kind of person no one would have remembered if he had ever attended a high school reunion. He never seemed to get his feet on the ground. I don't believe he ever held down a job. His social skills were a little skimpy and since his parents provided everything he needed, which wasn't very much, he never needed to strive to succeed in the world. He had limited *get up* and not very much *go*. He apparently shaved and bathed occasionally but I suspect that most of his clothes were hand-me-downs from his father. At the age of 30 they finally kicked him out of the main house but only 200 feet away to the self-contained cabin at the back of the property near the tree line. It had power, water, a wood stove, and a bathroom, but was pretty much a very spartan one room bachelor pad. His mom still did much of his cooking, washing, and bought his groceries so there was little need for him to do anything for himself. It was kind of lonely out there in his cabin so one day he took in a stray dog. That gave him something to do and for the first time he had a purpose in life so he adopted a few more. He especially liked big dogs and as long as he only had a few he could pack them into the cab of his hand me down pickup truck when he bought them in for routine veterinary care. When you saw the truck from behind, it looked like there were four big guys all squeezed into the cab but three of them had especially large or long floppy ears. He could give you the whole life's history of each of his dogs and was surprisingly knowledgeable about their medical issues and needs. However, I'm not sure if he could even name the governor of the state or speak intelligently about any social or political issues. His life was filled with *just getting by* and his growing family of dogs.

Eventually Mom and Dad passed on and Jed inherited the estate and could move back into the main house. His parents had worked hard and been rather frugal so the house was paid for and Jed was left with a fairly sizable financial nest egg to carry him on through life. His needs were few so money did not seem to be an issue. His mother had trained him well so by watching for specials and saving coupons he was able to keep his family well fed and groomed. And he kept collecting more dogs. He had started with a giant Great Dane cross who ate four cans a day and must have weighed 130lb Then came a giant slobbery Mastiff who was even bigger than the Great Dane. He then stepped down to a hound cross whose bay could be heard for miles and some sort of a German Shepherd mix with droopy ears and a tennis ball fetish. Then back up to a slow walking Saint Bernard drooly cross and then a big white hairy Newfoundland. He bought an old Ford Estate station wagon to transport his family but it wasn't long till even that was not big enough.

Some of the dogs were prone to wandering and he inevitably got complaints from neighbors. There is not room for an unlimited number of dogs even in a fairly large house, so it became necessary to chain some of them outside to trees or attaching them to a long clothes lines allowing them to run back and forth. He realized this was not an ideal means of caring for his friends so he eventually splurged and fenced in a large area of pasture where his herd could be free to bark, excavate large holes, chase their tails, check out each other's butts, or just sleep in the sun or shade. Jed's one room cabin became a giant dog house with heat, light and running water. He built bunk beds all across one wall to accommodate the dog's down time.

Dogs can do a pretty impressive job of safely socializing with each other if there is no human intervention. It seems like dogs are more likely to act inappropriately when they are being protective or possessive of their owners. When the local animal shelter had a large dog that they could not place, they knew that they could call Jed and he could always find room for one more. He was good about making sure they were neutered or spayed and vaccinated and that their health needs were taken care of. But it was becoming more and more difficult to bring his guys in to the office.

One day he called in to make an appointment and we set aside two hours to take care of his herd. He came in the front door grinning at 2 PM and said. "I want everybody to come out and see what I've got." We all trooped after him out to the parking lot and there sat an ancient 50 passenger yellow school bus. He had put white paint over all the identifying lettering except for the word 'bus' and had crudely written with black permanent marker the word *'DOG* above it. All the windows were ratcheted down one or two notches and most of them had a dog head poking out. Jed said, "They almost have assigned seats. We can go out for a drive and most of them have their favorite seat to park in where they can slime or fog up the windows or stick their heads out if the weather is decemt." He even had a little foot stool by the folding front doors to help the older less agile dogs climb up the

106

steps. There was a large *no spill* water trough that Jed had designed located right behind the driver's seat. It was a good thing seat belts were not required for dogs. It was quite a sight to see the yellow ***DOG BUS*** traveling around on the county roads. He said, "I occasionally even stop at drive-in restaurants and order paper dishes of vanilla ice cream for everyone." I wonder how many gallons of Windex and rolls of paper towels it took to wash the drool and nose prints off of all of the 30 windows? At least they didn't leave left over lunch on the seats or floor.

Jed is pretty old now and doesn't drive much. I think his vision is a little shaky too. The surviving dogs aren't getting any younger either. There is a little pet cemetery back on a tree covered knob with painted white wooden crosses marking the graves of all his departed rescued friends. He bus hasn't moved in a few years and the left front tire is flat. The dead branches and fir needles on the roof look like a bad haircut. Jed has reverted back to the Ford wagon and we just do geriatric care on his family now. Jed says, "I'm not taking in any more additional dogs now. I need to be sure I outlive all my friends. I don't think anyone else would want to adopt them if I'm gone."

I miss seeing that old bus rumbling around the back roads.

THE LONGEST RIDE

Time, water, and weather are commanding irresistible forces of nature. Their combined energies finally defeated an old bridge high in the Cascade Mountains at a place called Dutch Miller Gap. Older bridges over mountain streams were typically constructed on site by dragging two logs over the stream and then nailing decking on top. The decking was made by splitting smaller logs in half and mounting them flat side up with a rounded bottom side seated in notches cut in the main stringers. The bridge in the extreme headwaters of the Waptus River was probably built by President Roosevelt's New Deal Civilian Conservation Corps crews during the Great Depression in the Years 1933 to 1942.

It had been a winter of very heavy snowfall with that area probably receiving 400 inches or 33 feet of total accumulation. As the snow packs, it forms a dense mass 10 to 12 feet deep. Anything in the way of the settling snow gets smashed and the tired rotten logs of this 20-foot bridge could not withstand the pressure and finally succumbed to the inevitable. When things began warming in the spring, snow melt commenced but a week

108

of hot weather caused significant flooding. Even the broken-backed bridge was carried off downstream and eventually over a waterfall never to be seen again.

This trail, being part of the Pacific Crest Trail, had a high priority so when the snow melted off, engineers hiked in to take measurements and design a new bridge. Ultimately, some of the materials were delivered by helicopter to the site and a construction crew hiked in to prepare the site and start construction. A few days before the final load of materials delivery, a fire broke out and the helicopter was needed for the firefighting effort elsewhere. So, the crew of six men was parked 16 miles up in the mountains with nothing to do. The problem was discussed and it was decided to use pack mules to deliver the needed materials.

Thus, began my longest ride. Starting in the dark at the government corrals about 4:30 in the morning we saddled the mules and loaded the timbers. The decking was 4 in thick, 12 in wide, and 6 feet long with each piece weighing about 50lbs. Each mule could carry four with two on each side. I had some help packing the mules and was headed up the trail long before the sun came up. It would be about 16 miles with 3000 feet elevation gain. The mules were steady and trailed well and we made good time. About 4 1/2 hours later we arrived at the construction site to be greeted by the raucous cheer of the construction crew. It didn't take long to unload so I loosened the cinches and quickly turned the string around and headed back down the mountain. Leo the mule was a good walker who could keep up with my saddle horse so I led him and just turned the other four mules lose to follow along behind. We trotted when the trail allowed and only about three and a half hours we were back at the trailhead. And what to do now? It was still early in the afternoon and there was some help available, so being young and foolish I put feed bags on the animals so they could refuel while we reloaded them with the remainder of the timbers. I was riding my personal saddle horse who was 17 hands tall. He was a little less eager when we remounted and headed back up the trail. Five hours later we were back up at the bridge site. Then the realization struck that I didn't have anything to sleep in and strangely nobody wanted a buddy in their sleeping bag. There was some burnt stew in the bottom of the pot leftover from dinner and after I gulping that down and filling my pockets with Oreo Cookies, I headed back down the trail in total darkness. There were some stretches where a misstep on the part of your horse would lead to double fatality. There was a river ford where if a horse went down in the dark there's no telling what the outcome would be. There were hooting owls, the crashes and snaps of branches being broken in the dark, deer jumping off the trail off into the bushes and also the usual compliment of sasquatches, lions, and rhinoceroses. A couple of times I nodded off but managed to catch myself before I fell out of the saddle. About 2 AM, I got back to the government corrals and unsaddled and watered and fed the horses. I was even too tired for another Oreo Cookie so I just crawled into the cab of the stock truck to sleep until morning. About 8:30 in the morning I was startled awake by someone pounding on the window. I got the rest of the day off to rest, refuel, check my butt for blisters, and recollect the events from the previous day. My horse, the five mules, and I had traveled well over 60 miles with an elevation change of 12 to 13,000 feet. I don't think even John Wayne had ever ridden that far in a day let alone pack and unpack 5 mules with two heavy loads. The new bridge is now 45 years old and seems to be holding up to whatever Mother Nature can throw at it.

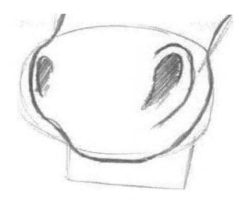

I SMELL YOU

Horses have an acute sense of smell; not as sensitive as a dog's but considerably better than a human being. When a horse grazes, it uses its senses of sight, taste, touch, and smell. The eyes and their green sensitive cones or color receptors help them sort out the subtle colors of their forage. Their amazing almost prehensile lips can feel the texture of the feed and even pluck out a single blade of grass from amongst inedible weeds. They can bite off the end of a thistle and adroitly maneuver it around so that the stickers point away in a safe direction and then chew and swallow it down. If they grab a clump of grass and it comes out with a root wad full of dirt, they sometimes bang the wad on the ground or their leg to clear the dirt or else just spit the whole clump out and look for a better one. Their sense of smell also helps them locate and identify favorite foods. When they are investigating something that is apparently safe but unknown, they often come up and sniff it carefully before further testing it with their lips.

Horses greet each other nose to nose to identify each other and probably even assess the attitude of the other by sniffing their breath and blowing puffs of air into the other horse's nostrils. Humans can greet their horses in the same way. You should approach the horse a little bit indirectly from the side because they do not see close up very well directly ahead. Once they have identified you, you can blow short puffs of air into their nostril and they reciprocate by puffing short warm breaths into your face. They smell like a warm salad. It is perhaps not wise to do this to a horse you don't know or especially a stallion.

A recently graduated veterinarian who worked for me learned this the hard way. He knew that blowing puffs of air into a horse's nose could to have a calming reassuring effect on the horse. We had been called to castrate a young stallion and I sent Robert out on a farm call to take care of it. George, the owner of the young stallion, had never married and was a little eccentric. He still lived with his parents and they all resided in an unfinished house that he was slowly building for his parents. He had completed enough of the construction to get a habitation permit and he was doing the finishing work as time and money were available. They had extra land and decided they needed some animals to graze among the pine trees. They got a few calves, two goats, and someone gave them an unbroken crossbred Arab stallion.

The horse was halter broken but had no other training. He was a pretty sorrel with a full blaze and four white stockings but had developed into quite a handful. The horse was more mischievous than he was dangerous but it is still a little intimidating to have an 800lb animal dancing on his hind legs trying to have a boxing match with you. The family decided it was time for an attitude adjustment. Robert drove down the winding 1/4-mile tree lined

112

lane and George was waiting. The horse galloped up bucking and kicking and investigated Robert over the top rail of the corral. While he was waiting for George to come back with a bucket of hot water and there was nothing better to do, Robert decided to blow puffs of air into the young stallion's nose. The stallion reciprocated and all seem to be going well until he opened his mouth and grabbed Robert by the chin with his impressive set of incisors. I suspect Robert pulled back instinctively while the stallion did not let go. The result was a horribly torn lower lip and chin. Needless to say, the decision to castrate the colt was delayed.

Veterinarians always have lots of bandage material so Robert and George bandaged the damage chin and Robert drove on down to the emergency room at the local hospital. This was late on a Friday afternoon. After waiting the typical hour-and-a-half for help, since he did not appear to be dying, the emergency physician examined him and said, "Nice bandaging job but this is something that needs a plastic surgeon to repair. I'll make some calls and see what we can arrange. After another hour of waiting it was learned that the plastic surgeon took three-day weekends and would not be available until Tuesday. What to do? The doctor said that the delay would be okay as long as they could keep the wound clean and moist.

Veterinarians like to use something called a wet to dry bandage where a saline saturated pad is placed over a wound which is then covered by a dry pad. Robert, who of course had a little difficulty articulate in his words, suggested this to the doctor who said, "That that would probably be fine."

It was my weekend off and we were out camping so Robert had no way of informing me of his medical predicament. I guess veterinarians were tougher in those days so with the help of our veterinary technician he kept his chin bandaged all weekend and

Another Day

proceeded to even handle a few emergencies over the weekend. I got back Sunday evening and after checking in, learned of Roberts dilemma. I very generously told him that, "I suppose you can take Monday off if you really need to."

He managed to form a distorted smile and said, "I would be grateful for that." On Tuesday the plastic surgeon put Robert's face back together again. The edges of the tear were rather ragged so they had to trim away some of the damaged flesh. In fact, they had to trim away more than a quarter inch of skin from his lower lip and chin. Weeks later after healing had taken place, we were able to accuse him of being a little tight-lipped. In the hands of a skilled plastic surgeon, pretty amazing results can be achieved. After the surgery there was, of course, a shortage of skin that over time stretched to accommodate the body's needs.

Robert cultured a beard for a few years but in time the scar was almost imperceptible. He was wiser but none the worse for wear. In addition to accusing him of being "*tight-lipped*" we told him it was probably not a good idea to "*blow smoke*" in somebody's face and that he was probably full of *hot air*.

The following week we discussed finishing the job on the colt and Robert with his lopsided smile said, "I'll do it. A cowboy never leaves a job unfinished. I need to show that young stud that I'm still the boss." Where would the world be without testosterone?

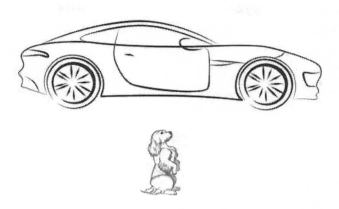

PRINCE

There was a young Saudi Prince who, like other Arab men of royal descent, had a long complicated five-part name that delineated his heritage, described his virtues, indicated his tribe, and defined his relationship with Allah. Wanting to have the appearance of being more modern, he said, "Just call me Prince." Nevertheless, he enjoyed wearing the keffiyeh (headdress) and thoub (white robe) traditional to Saudi males. The royal family was, of course, rich beyond all imagination. Employment was not an issue so to keep from being totally bored, he had numerous hobbies. One was falconry where he raised raptors to hunt birds and small desert mammals. He also owned a stable of camels and was involved with camel racing. A young man's life would not be complete without some sort of overpowered motor vehicle so he had a fleet of dune buggies for racing out in the desert sand with his many cousins.

It should not come as a surprise to learn that the Prince Omar was a little eccentric. He liked many of the same things that you and I do but often for strange and unusual reasons. For example,

115

who does not like toast with rich butter melted on top? You and I might say we like toast and butter. Our prince, however, liked bright colors and so he ordered toast and color when he went out to a restaurant for breakfast. Needless to say, the poor waitresses were baffled by his unusual request and the spoiled prince became indignant and berated them and made huge ugly scenes. Eventually, law enforcement was typically involved, but to no one's surprise the prince, being well protected by his royal family name, never seemed to suffer any ill consequences for his idiocy.

Strangely, the prince was very fond of Cocker Spaniel dogs. He had a kennel full of blond purebred English Cocker Spaniels There was a royal kennel master for grooming and daily care of the dogs. You and I might like these dogs to run, fetch, roll over and do other doggy things. The prince, however, didn't like them for the reasons you and I might. He liked them for the sound they made when they were panting. So, he didn't call them his Cocker Spaniels. He called them his Panties. When he came home in the evening after a day of philandering, he liked to get in his Maserati sports car and drive up and down his long royal driveway. He would take the dogs down to the end and chase them from the driver's seat of his car all the way back to the kennel just so he could hear them pant. A certain amount of running is fun for a dog but there is a reasonable limit. Cocker Spaniels, after all, are not renowned for their racing prowess. The prince did this day after day and ran the poor little dogs ragged. Can dogs communicate with each other and plan things out, such as for revenge? Who knows, but one hot day after the dogs had suffered through this game several times, they finally had enough and when the prince got out of his car to put the dogs back in their kennel the Cocker Spaniels chased him up against a wall and the prince got eaten by his Panties.

REJECTED

The shortest distance

Between two points

Is not always a straight line.

Like many people, after completing a university degree, I was uncertain what my next life stage step should be. The Army quickly resolved that for me because my low draft lottery number got drawn and I had lost my educational deferment. This was one national lottery you didn't want to win. About that same time, I had a life changing epiphany. While sailing a small dinghy on Lake Washington north of the Evergreen Point Floating Bridge, I realized that a career as a veterinarian would be a good fit for my broad-based scientific interests and love of animals.

Off I went to fulfill my military obligation and when that Vietnam period of my life concluded, I mailed my application to the WSU College of Veterinary Medicine. I waited expectantly for the return letter and one day it finally arrived. My wife and I opened the letter with trepidation. The air disappeared from the room when I found I had been rejected. I had degrees in mathematics and chemistry but lacked many of the prerequisite classes such as biology, zoology, bacteriology, nutrition, and genetics. At the time, it hadn't seemed like such a big deal to me that I haven't fulfilled most of the basic educational requirements for a veterinary school applicant. So, what to do now? We were in an emotional quandary when I mustered out of the Army. With my discharge papers and a large brown envelope full of $20 bills in hand from my last Army payday, we drove across the country from Massachusetts to Washington State. The concentration of driving and the beauty and expanse of our great country provided a temporary respite from the concern about my future. It was a great trip. We stopped in Algonquin Provincial Park in Canada and listened to the wolves howling as we snuggled in our Army sleeping bags in our Army tent. After driving across the endless flat croplands of North Dakota the hoodoos of the Badlands of South Dakota suddenly appeared. Grand Teton National Park made me want to come back in the winter time with my skis to enjoy Jackson Hole. Then came Yellowstone National Park. We arrived on the first spring day when tourists were allowed to enter the park. The previous year they had closed the park garbage dumps which had been a source of food for a large number of the Yellowstone bears. There were hungry bears and idiot photographers with the resulting traffic jams everywhere. We watched a mother moose try and get her wobbly hours-old calf across a small rushing stream. and buffalo babies cavort in grassy meadows. Finally, we traversed Glacier National Park on the Going to the Sun Highway and were on the home stretch back to Washington State. In a moment of inspiration, we decided to take

118

a slight detour through Pullman, WA to look at the WSU campus and the vet school but we really had no particular plan in mind. One of the main buildings, McCoy Hall, was open and I decided to go inside and look around. I saw a professorial looking gentleman coming down the hall wearing a white lab coat and making a spur of the moment decision, I asked if he had a moment to answer some questions for me. He politely stopped and smiled and said, "The school is closed for the summer but what do you want to know." I quickly explained a little bit of my background and the fact that I had just got out of the Army only to discover my application to the vet school had been turned down. With his hand on his chin in a contemplatively manner, he paused for a moment and said, "I don't know if I'm supposed to do this but I can't think of any reason why not. What was your name?" I told him and he said, "Well, it happens that I was the chairman of the admissions committee and I thought I recognized your story and name. As perhaps you know we accepted 60 applications. Two of them decided to go to other schools and so two alternate applicants were accepted to fill out the class. What do you suppose your number was?"

I said, "I have no idea."

He said, "You were number 63. Numbers 1 through 62 got in and number 63 didn't. We looked at your background, your grades, and your degrees and decided that you were an acceptable risk. So, what you need to do is go to school for another year, get good grades in those missing prerequisite classes, and apply again next year. Do that and you will be in next year's class."

Now, I could look ahead and see a light at the end of the tunnel. Hard work is manageable if there is a worthwhile journey's end.

That summer I worked for a few months in a local vegetable processing freezing plant and then began my job as Wilderness Ranger for the US Forest Service. In the fall we moved to Pullman and rented a small house next door to the elementary school where my wife got a job teaching second grade. I took zoology, genetics, nutrition, bacteriology, and the only chemistry class that I had never taken, biochemistry. I studied hard but we also took time to hunt, fish, camp, and ski. I got a 4.0 GPA and, in the fall of 1970, entered the WSU College of Veterinary Medicine class of 1974.

And so, began the next day of the rest of my life.

KEEP ON TRUCKIN'

It was a nice enough little truck. I bought it from a local dealer when my older four-wheel drive S10 Blazer had a cardiac arrest and resuscitation failed! The price was right on this plain Jane two-wheel drive F-150 short box with a V8 and an automatic transmission. My granny would have loved it in her younger years. It took me two years to realize that I had made a serious mistake. The first two winters had been mild with the occasional snow quickly melting off. This winter, however, was different. Snow came early and deep and then cold weather settled in, resulting in icy ruts everywhere. Just as calving season was beginning, snow storm followed snow storm and I was constantly on the road to assist with bovine obstetrics. Long potholed ranch lanes, barnyards, and gravel country roads off into nearby forested canyons became a two-wheel drive vehicle's biggest nightmare. The little truck couldn't get out of its own way. The light rear end meant that you could not get traction even with the box full of sandbags. It was embarrassing to ask the rancher to give you a push just to get out of the barnyard. The final blow came one day after a 4-inch snowfall when I had to chain up the truck four different times. How happy I was when spring finally came and the ice melted off. I resolved to correct my mistake and get a vehicle more suited to my needs.

I looked online and found a low mileage four-wheel drive Ford Ranger that looked like a good possibility. It was at a high-volume dealership at the south end of Lake Washington. The young salesman was an arrogant know-it-all who was nevertheless unable to answer many of the basic questions about the truck. I liked it and strongly considered buying it anyway but I'm the kind of person who likes to check things over and consider everything carefully before making a final decision. I said, "Let me think it over and get back to you."

He said, "What will it take to close the deal today."

I countered, "Give me more for my old truck and lower the price on the Ranger."

He eagerly replied, "Let me talk to the head salesman and I'll get right back with you." They took my keys so they could *check over my old truck* and put me in a room with a coffee machine, a water cooler, and a pile of old magazines.

There was also a young mother with two small children waiting there. I heard the door click *locked* when the salesman departed. I sat there for a while expecting the salesman to return but nothing happened. I asked the young mother how long she had been there and she looked at her watch and said, "It's been 45 minutes now. I wonder what is going on."

I tried to be patient for another 15 minutes but still no one showed up. Since the door was locked, I banged on the window and was initially ignored. Finally, someone came over to see what the commotion was. I shouted, "If there isn't someone here to unlock this door and let us out in one minute, I'm going to call

911 and report a kidnapping." There was a very startled look on the person's face and she quickly hurried away.

In 30 seconds, my young smart ### salesman was back asking what the problem was. I replied, "You know exactly what the problem is. You have had us locked up in this room for over an hour just letting us stew in our juices".

I said, "I'm out of here." I told the young mother, "Surely you can find another dealership to meet your needs who will treat you with respect and does not use high pressure sales tactics to close a deal."

She looked at me with a frightened look on her face and said, "But they have my car keys."

Just then the head salesman arrived and introduced himself holding paperwork ready to close the deal. I took a deep breath and tried to cool down. With an eyelid twitching and an upper lip quivering, I stood very close to him and looked at him right in the eye and said, "Before you do anything with me, you're going to return this lady's car keys." The look on his face indicated that he realized that I realized that this was part of their sales tactic. The lady looked at me with a smile of relief and gathered up her two small children and fled out the door. I had done my homework and knew what my old truck was worth and had a pretty good idea what would be reasonable price for the Ford Ranger.

The offer was reasonable so with considerable reluctance, I said, "I would like to buy the truck but only under certain conditions." We'd had to jump the battery to get the truck started so I said, "I want a new battery."

The tires were worn out and I demanded, "I want a new set of tires." There was also only one set of keys which were specially equipped with a chip to prevent theft.

123

They agreed to all these things and I said, "I will be back tomorrow to pick up the truck." They also had agreed to let me pay for it with my credit card since this was how I paid for all my business expensed. I noticed when I went out to get in my old truck that had it had not been moved. Obviously, nobody had come out to *examine* it.

When I came back the next day the Ranger sat exactly where we left at the previous day. It was evident that nothing had been done and they wanted me to take the truck as it was and bring it back later to fulfill my requests.

I sat for a few minutes before I located the head salesman and stated, "Yesterday you promised that you would have this truck ready for me to pick up today and it is not ready. I've wasted 5 hours and driven 250 miles. The whole process has been an extreme pain in the ass for me. As you recall you let me pay for the truck on my credit card. Now listen very carefully. I am not going to repeat this. It is now 4:15 in the afternoon. You have exactly one hour to do the work as promised or I will get on my cell phone and call my credit card company and have the transaction cancelled. And, if you lock me in that room again, I will immediately call the Renton Police Department. Are we clear?"

The head salesman got red in the face and puffed up his chest. I repeated, "Are we clear sir or are you deaf or are you just plain stupid?"

He started to say something but closed his mouth and finally said, "We will get it done, Sir." After an hour, I had four new tires and a battery but he explained that their technician who coded the keys was on vacation and they had been unable to get me an additional spare key. He promised to call my home town Ford dealership and arrange to have them take care of it for me.

At that point I was still mad but nevertheless felt that I had made a reasonable business transaction.

I gradually relaxed during the two-hour drive home in the dark. I didn't know anything about yoga or meditation but I tried some deep breathing since nobody was watching. Then a courteous fellow driver notified me that I had no tail lights. The vehicle had supposedly been *safety checked*. When I finally got home, I had a glass of milk and three Oreo Cookies. The next morning, I discovered that the night before when I went to bed, I was so tired that I had failed to get my body *between* the sheets on our bed. It only got worse when my wife commented, "Nice truck, but I really don't like the color."

The little truck served me well but I subsequently discovered that they had installed the new battery with only one tie-down bolt, a new front tire was out of balance, and they never called the local Ford dealership to get me a second key. Fearing what I might say or do, I decided to let sleeping dogs lie and found a replacement battery tie-down bolt in the junkyard, got the tire balanced at no cost at my local friendly tire shop, and paid my local Ford dealership $135 for a microchipped Ford ignition key. I guess I would have to reluctantly admit that the final score for this ridiculous exasperating game was:

High Volume Dealership:	3
Mixed Practice Veterinarian:	1
Lesson learned:	GET IT IN WRITING!
Truthful admission.	A GUY HAS TO HAVE A TRUCK

BIG BLONDS

Have you ever visited British Columbia's capital city of Victoria? It's situated on the beautiful scenic southern tip of Vancouver Island so the only realistic way to visit is by ferry boat. With its bustling Inner Harbor and iconic Empress Hotel building, it feels like a visit to London. There are double decker bus tours, frequent rain, some right-hand drive taxis with boots and bonnets, and lots of bicycles. One unique way to see the sights is by horse-drawn wagons. Capital City Tally Ho harnesses two giant Percheron horses to a wagon which holds 10 or 12 tourists on bench seats. It is a seasonal tourist activity so there is a need to care for the 44 giant horses in the off season when they are not in service. Keeping them stabled and fed is an endless and expensive proposition. After all they only eat about 40lb of hay per day. Consequently, for the winter, they were transported to an area and climate where they could be more economically kept as a free herd and fed outdoors. They were packed 12 at a time into a large stock trailer (that's over 12 tons of horse) and hauled cross the Washington British Columbia border to my hometown for the winter. They were turned out into a 40-acre pasture where they grazed as long as forage was available. When serious winter weather with its snow arrived, the caregiver would hitch two of the horses to an old wooden hay wagon and drive around the field pitch forking off hay for the horses to feed on. The horses had an original issue auto pilot system and could move the wagon around with only voice commands. Unlike Siri, they were unable to answer questions. The winter weather could be cold but the low humidity made it tolerable for the horses to survive in the open with no shelter other than a few large trees. They became very hairy and in fact so well insulated that new snow sometimes did not even melt from their backs. I occasionally saw them during the winter months for minor health issues but my interaction with them peaked in the spring when it was time for them to travel back to Canada for their summer non-vacation in Victoria. But to travel across the border they needed a health certificate and a test for an infectious disease called equine infectious anemia (Coggins). Each animal had to be identified and described and sketched on paper and then have a blood sample taken for the prescribed test. The problem was that they were all very blond sorrel Percheron horses which were hard to distinguish one from another even to the trained eye. They all had white stockings and blazes on their heads with the white fading into the sorrel color so there were not any clear lines of color demarcation. Horses, like people, have cowlicks or whorls in their hair coat. (Or maybe they have horselicks.) It could become necessary to even identify the location and direction on these whorls to distinguish one horse from another. An appointment would be made each spring of the year for an all-day horse portrait drawing event. Each of the horses had to be caught, identified, and a blood sample taken. (Since that time the USDA has accepted photographs for identification purposes making the task much easier).

It was quite a sight to see 44 horses come galloping into the corral from the distant reaches of the pasture. You didn't want to be standing near the gate when this thundering herd came snorting past. They weren't pulling the Budweiser wagon either. Once in the corral the horses would be squealing, flattening ears, and threatening to kick as they jockeyed to maintain their social position within the herd. It's also interesting to be an insignificant human trying to poke a needle into the neck of a posturing 2000lb steam engine. Fortunately, in spite of the excitement of the moment, the horses were well trained and had respect for their puny fragile human handlers. A well-placed stomp or kick could prove disastrous to a two-legged participant. Eventually, they were all examined for health issues, a blood sample taken, and paperwork completed for the return back into Canada. The samples were sent off to a diagnostic lab for testing and then the horses could be loaded into their truck to cross the border at Blaine into British Columbia and then travel by ferry to their summer home in Victoria. I have sometimes wondered if horses got seasick. I don't believe that the customs agents at the border were required to do any whole-body cavity searches for drugs or contraband on the horses.

The owner of the business, Bruce, with his heavy English accent, liked American Olympia Beer and we would always have a twelve pack on hand so we could tip back one or two brews when he was here to collect his horses. He would call from the border on his way here from Victoria so that we could meet him at the ranch to begin our processing. His personality was as big as the horses so his levity and banter helped make time pass.

We occasionally visited Vancouver Island in the summer to visit my parents who vacationed at the famous salmon fishing community of Campbell River. We sometimes passed through Victoria on our way north to Campbell River. It was fun seeing the horses I attended in Ellensburg pulling wagons around the streets of Victoria. Horses can only pull a heavy wagon for about 3 hours and then need to be returned to the stable to be swapped out for a fresh team. The number of wagons and the necessity of giving horses days off required having at least 40 horses plus a few additional spare tires.

Times and circumstances change and eventually the fee to cross at the border became prohibitive and the Tally Ho horses stopped wintering in central Washington. It was cheaper to over winter them in British Columbia rather than haul them back and forth across the border twice a year. Ten years passed and my family was growing up and expanding. I had my own son and two instant daughters from a second marriage. They would soon be out of high school and dispersed so the family decided to do a Disney World vacation in Florida and they thoughtfully allowed me to come along.

We saw the Orlando sights and visited Universal Studios and Disney World. As the vacation was ending, we decided to dedicate the last day to the Epcot Center. It was a large acreage with pavilions dedicated to national and commercial areas of interest from around the world. It was like a permanent World's Fair. Sponsors included such companies as Exxon, Kraft, and Nestle and countries such as China, Japan, Mexica, France, Germany, and Canada. It was sweaty hot and humid so we ducked into the air-conditioned Canadian Pavilion to cool down. There was a display area and then you passed into a large IMAX type theater. Scenes from Canada were displayed on a 360-degree screen so that things in motion seem to pass around you and even right over your head. The effect could be a little vertigo inducing so there were railings to hang onto so that people in the audience wouldn't tip over. You sat in the cockpit of a screaming military jet as it screamed between peaks in the Canadian Rockies. You crouched on the dirt floor of an arena as the Royal Canadian Mounted Police in their precision equine Musical Ride passed right over the top of your head, and hunkered down as your raft descended a rapid and you got drenched with spray.

Finally, you relaxed on the cushioned seat of a horse-drawn wagon as it traveled through the streets of downtown Victoria. I couldn't help myself and whispered loudly to my family, "That's Harry and Charles from the Tally Ho horses!" We had traveled 3000 miles across our great country only to see two of the horses I saw every spring back at Washington State. They were much better groomed, had braids in their mane and tail instead of cockleburs, had little tassels on their bridle headstall, and were prancing along like they were pulling the Queen in her royal carriage. The Disney phrase *It's a Small World After All* came to mind.

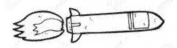

UNGUIDED MISSLE

Don Brown was a horse breeder. He bred paint horses from foundation stock quarter horse bloodlines. His horse knowledge was extensive, his horses were spectacular, and his pocketbook had a padlock on it. You had to admire his horsemanship and the quality of his animals but getting paid for your services could sometimes be a drawn-out uncertain process. Was he just tight with his money or was money just a little tight? I never really had an answer for that question but his *accounts due* grew year by year.

My wife said, "He has truly spectacular stallions. Why don't we breed my bay mare Ribbons in trade for his bill?"

We ruminated on this for a few days and then it occurred to me, "If we breed your mare, what are you going to ride for those two years?" You can, of course, ride a pregnant mare but our riding style was a little bit extreme for a pregnant mare and once she foaled, we would have to leave the baby home alone.

You could almost see the lightbulbs switch on and off in her brain and she said definitively, "Well, then we will just trade for one of his horses."

My wife was good friends with Don's wife and I think that greased the bargaining process. We traded for Diamond, a golden sorrel quarter horse mare with a small perfect star (Diamond) on her forehead and bloodlines tracing directly back to a famous Quarter Horse named Poco Bueno. She had been purchased direct from the King Ranch in Texas in hopes that she would produce paint babies. Her babies were spectacular but never showed any color. They are called **Solid Paint Bred** or **Paints That Ain't** by Paint Horse breeders. Thus, Don was more than glad to exchange Diamond for his vet bill. Being a horse trader by nature he easily came up with a long list of all her fine qualities one of which was that she was well broken and would be safe for a preteenager daughter. Such did not prove to be the case. The horse was a finely tuned American muscle car. Eager, very willing, tremendously powerful, and extremely athletic. It appeared that she had only had some basic training before being turned into a baby factory. Obviously, she was not the horse for a young inexperienced rider and by default she became my project. She was fun, willing, and a quick learner, but proved to be much more athletic than her rider. All too frequently she could be observed grazing quietly alongside the trail while I was still suspended in midair, waiting to fall, at her previous location. Fortunately, my wife was usually the only person to observe my unseating.

During this period of my career, I had been unable to find a sufficiently qualified associate so the only way to get time off for myself and family was to *Get Out of Dodge.* If I was home, I felt obligated to answer the phone and was thus never really able to escape. One of our favorite escape mechanisms was to ride mountain trails with our horses. Typically, I would work until noon on Saturdays and rush home. My wife would have lunches ready, the trailer hooked up, and the horses loaded. All I had to do was put on my cowboy hat and face and get behind the wheel. This was our plan one Saturday afternoon. The cool temperatures would be perfect for the horses who had to do most of the work. We liked to use the horses for exploring and if you plodded along slowly you never got very far and weren't able to see new country. Consequently, when we rode, we rode hard. Once the horses were shed out and legged up, our goal, within reason, was to cover as much ground as possible. The horses loved mountain trails and when the grade and terrain allowed, we often traveled at a fast trot. They seemed to understand our philosophy and if they could look ahead and see a smooth trail with an easy grade, they automatically shifted into a mile eating trot on their own accord without a cue from us.

That particular day we planned to ride in the Buck Meadows area on the Hereford Meadows and Shoestring Lake Trails. The route passed in and out of deep shady timber, crossed several streams that provided drinking water for the horses and dog, and traversed long open sunlit grassy hillsides where deer or elk were sometimes spotted.

As we arrived in the parking area a mule deer doe eased out of the meadow into the tree line. I suspect she had a spotted fawn hidden in a thicket somewhere nearby. We could hear a Townsend's Warbler singing from the top branches of a spruce tree. The trail started out in previously logged second growth with a smooth easy uphill grade. The horses were so eager to get going that mounting was tricky with them moving off even before you had your right leg in the stirrup. Our dog was already

200 feet up the trail barking impatiently at our slow progress. Soon we were in old growth Douglas fir as we paralleled a cool quiet stream. Surely there must have been a trout hiding behind every rock and underneath every root. The trail now began climbing steadily and my mare was traveling mostly on autopilot. She climbed enthusiastically until she needed a break and then stopped on her own accord. When she was rested enough to continue, she self-started and off we went. After about an hour and a half we were 5 miles into the ride and it was time for a snack break. We dismounted and haltered the horses so they could graze while we drank some water. I also needed an Oreo cookie. There were a few large grasshoppers buzzing about in the sun sounding like miniature two cycle motorcycles revving their engines.

Again, the horses danced about impatiently as we remounted to continue with our ride. The trail eased on downhill through some wide-sweeping turns. It was kind of a rough jarring ride but we let the horses stretch into an extended trot and we even leaned into the slightly banking corners. I typically stood up in the stirrups to let my legs take the beating instead of my rear end. With one hand on my mare's neck to maintain my balance, I glanced ahead into a small clearing. I think my horse and I simultaneously observed the scene unfolding in front of us. There were about 30 elk with their calves bedded down in that clearing quietly chewing their cud. Our sudden arrival put them all in flight mode and they scrambled to their feet and disappeared into the brush.

My mare locked up all four wheels and skidded almost to a standstill before she whirled and was instantly pointed back up the trail at a full trot. Not having a seatbelt, Super Glue, or Velcro on my butt, I suddenly became a launched unguided missile. Out of my peripheral vision I sensed, while I was still in mid-air, that

134

my mare was already accelerating in the opposite direction. Somehow, I managed to tuck my body slightly thus protecting my head and landing on my left side. I lay there totally stunned for about 10 seconds. When I lifted my head to see if I was dead, I looked around and discovered I had slid between two large boulders and my head rested within a few inches of a log. When my horse whirled, my wife was right behind her and she was just able to gather up a rein and keep her from potentially retracing our route all the way back to the trailer. It would have been a long walk. The temperature had been cool enough that I had on a light jacket that protected me from serious road rash.

When I finally stood up and sat on the log, there was still a cloud of dust stirred up by all the confusion. I was relatively young and, of course, believed that I was an indestructible male, so I could never be seen sporting a riding helmet. I did pause to reconsider that decision when I pulled pine needles out of my hair, shook pebbles from my ears, and left a slimy dirty deposit on my handkerchief. We could still hear the elk crashing through the brush and the quiet squeaky bleating sounds of the calves.

Horses seem to have an uncanny internal compass. The ride that day was a loop where we were able to return back to the truck by a different route. Even though the horses had never been on that trail before, they knew that we had gradually turned and were on the right general compass heading to get back to our starting point. No encouragement was required for them to proceed at their fastest walk. A short distance ahead the trail crossed the headwaters of Manastash Creek via a long narrow rustic bridge. It was a good place to stop and wash the dirt off of my hands and face. The snow melt water was headache cold when I sloshed my head in it.

Can lightning strike twice in the same place? Well almost. About 2 miles ahead we met the 30-cow elk herd and their babies again. They heard us coming and waited politely off to the side of the trail until we passed. The horses saw them and were a little concerned but this time my mare and I were ready and communicating on the same frequency so there was no repeat launching of the unguided-missile. The rest of the ride was uneventful. We encountered no polar bears, hippopotami, great white sharks, or giraffes, and if there was a Sasquatch watching us, we were unaware. We did see a spotted mule deer fawn bounce across the trail just before we got back to the truck.

Are cowboys, tough, skilled, lucky, dumb, or just have a surplus of testosterone? A little bit of each I suppose.

HISTORY OF HORSES IN KITTITAS VALLEY

Known equine ancestry starts with Eohippus, a 30lb dog sized grazing animal with 3 toes. Over a period of 50 million years it eventually evolved into Equus simplicidens, remains of which were found in Idaho in 1928. This modern horse developed in North America during the Pleistocene epoch (3.5 – 2.5 million years ago) and it migrated over the Bering land bridge into Asia and Europe. Now, fast forward to the last incursion of the Cordilleran Ice Sheet into North America of 15,000 to 12,000 years ago. Due to changing climate (I doubt that this one was caused by man), and hunting pressure, the modern Equus, like the wooly mammoth, became extinct in North America. However, it had survived and prospered in Asia and Europe.

The silk road was important for trade but it also brought horses from Europe back to Asia where they were further refined. The Chinese needed them to combat the horse mounted Mongolians. Horses had been missing from the Americas for 12 to 15,000 years until Christopher Columbus reintroduced them during his exploratory voyages to the Caribbean. On his second voyage he brought 25 horses from Spain to Cuba and Hispaniola (Haiti and Dominican Republic) (He also brought smallpox for which the "Indians" traded back tobacco and syphilis). The first horse breeding colony was established in Cuba. One reference with genetic documentation says these horses were of Sorraia and Galicia breeding named after those regions of Spain. Later explorers brought more horses and in 1519 Cortez established a breeding colony on the island of Hispaniola which he used as a base of operations to explore and plunder Mexico.

The remnants of these horses (16 brought by Cortez) became the Galiceno breed. They were not selectively bred but rather bred freely more along the lines of survival of the fittest. They are short (12 – 13.5 hands), small (600 – 750lb), short backed, narrow but deep chested, usually solid colored or roan, and may have a dorsal stripe, shoulder cross, and zebra striped legs (primitive markings). Blood lines have been found to be surprisingly pure with little evidence of interbreeding. The Spanish Colonial Horse was said to be clannish staying together as a herd and avoiding mixing with other horses. They were used for transportation, dray, pack, and in the mines by the colonial explorers and settlers. By the 1600's as these horses were released, stolen, or escaped, they developed into the Spanish Mustang including the Kiger of Oregon, the Sulfur of SW Utah, and the Pryor Mountain of Montana.

In 1539 De Soto brought horses to Florida which developed into the Florida Cracker Horse so named for the

138

"crack" of the bullwhip wielded by its rider while herding cattle. Spanish rancheros had thousands of horses and the Spanish government established laws forbidding horse ownership by Indians. However, the Apache and Navaho had acquired horses and were excellent horsemen by the mid 1600's. They traded with the plains Comanche who, realizing their value, became adept at raiding Mexican rancheros. The horses were free ranging, easily rounded up, and may have been stolen at the rate of 30,000 per year.

Within 50 years the horse had spread north to the Shoshone, Crow, Flatheads and Nez Perce and thus our local Yakamas. Native American culture made a quantum leap in a few short years from a seasonal tribal foot migration to horse based. By 1730, in our region, the Nez Perce had become proficient horsemen. By 1760 horses could be found as far north as the Calgary region of western Canada. In 1814 a fur trader named Alexander Ross rode over Manastash Ridge into the Kittitas Valley to trade for horses and stumbled upon an enormous gathering of Indians. They may have numbered 10,000 and were encamped over a 6-mile area from the mouth of Naneum Canyon to Cariboo Creek. There may have been 3 horses for every Indian. Our valley was one of the few places where camas bulbs, kouse (known as biscuit root or Lomatium), and bitter root could be found in harvestable quantities. Tribes from the Great Plains, coastal Washington, British Columbia interior, Nez Perce, and the many sub tribes of the Yakamas were all present for trading, horse racing, games, food gathering, councils, dancing, and singing.

Apparently if you know where to look, there are still signs of their horse racing track. In 1859 James Kinney came to an area in Yakima and Benton counties between the Yakima and Columbia Rivers and observed the knee-high lush waving grass and large herds of wild horses and said, "This surely is a horse heaven." Thus, the name, the Horse Heaven Hills. The Kittitas Valley eventually turned to fenced pastures and hay production and the Horse Heavens, Palouse and Columbia Basin turned to grain

The Spanish mustang line has been greatly diluted by other breeds turned loose or escaped and all are in peril of suffering and starvation. They have exceeded the carrying capacity of their grazing ranges because of overpopulation, range degradation, or drought. There is no one solution pleasing to all concerned individuals.

WESTERN SEAFOOD

There's an old western tradition of mutual assistance among cattle ranchers. Many are smaller operators where the only affordable available labor is provided by family members. There are times when more bodies are needed and the ranchers take turns helping each other out; kind of like a barn raising. One such occasion is the working of the spring calf crop. Once all the calves are on the ground, they need to be vaccinated, branded, and the bull calves need an attitude adjustment (castration). Neighboring cattlemen and their families gather at each other's ranch to get this work done. Some enjoy doing it the old fashion way from horseback where a calf is roped from the herd and moved out to where the ground crew does the branding, vaccinating, and castrating. Most use modern cattle handling squeezes to individually control the calves while the tasks are finished. The crew moves from ranch to ranch over the course of a weekend and is culminated with a barbecue and *oyster* feed at the final stop. For the uninitiated, *oysters* are the bull calves' testicles which have been surgically removed and saved for the party. The ranchers and their adolescent assistants are working out in the corrals while the wives are preparing for the big picnic late in the afternoon. Old family recipes are resurrected for the preparation and cooking of the *Rocky Mountain Oysters*.

My son's best friend was the son of one of these cattle ranchers and I was the veterinarian who was called when services were required, so we were invited to this traditional annual event. It was a hot late summer weekend; the last before school started in the fall. If Mike eventually inherited his father's operation, he would be the fourth generation to live in the old farm house. The barn timbers were still held together with wooden pegs and the corrals were built out of posts and rails hauled out of the nearby forests. They were old but in good repair and very functional. Even though modern cattle working equipment was available, they had agreed for this final ranch to do it the old-fashioned way. They brought their favorite roping horse and took turns roping calves the traditional way. The smell of wood smoke was on the air from the fire to keep the branding irons glowing red. There was lots of good-natured ribbing when a cowboy missed with his loop and there were thick clouds of dust and dirty sweat streaked faces. Basically, for this event they were too many cowboys, too many horses, too many dogs, and too many young wannabe cowboys with hats one size too big for their heads each trying to prove his cowboy skills and document his masculinity. It was chaos but fun and it was impossible to find a face without a big smile and white teeth showing through the corral grime. Cowboy surgery can be a little crude and slightly unsanitary but it's been successful for hundreds of years so I diplomatically kept my medical advice to myself.

The wives and daughters were in the kitchen finishing the salads and garden vegetable side dishes and the homemade pies were cooling on the windowsill. Checkered oilcloth tablecloths were covering the picnic tables set up under the weeping willows in the front yard. Two huge rump roasts were slowly tuning on the spit over an applewood fire.

When the work was done and the cattle were turned out to pasture, the ranchers and their young helpers scrubbed the worst of the dirt off at the horse water tank and totally trashed the hostess's white towels when they dried off. Each rancher had brought his own *oysters* which had been carefully prepared by his wife. (Not all ranch wives necessarily enjoyed this task). These delicacies were all added to the communal pot and they were prepared as appetizers and hors d'oeuvres before the traditional main meal. Usually they were dipped in egg batter, covered with seasoned bread crumbs, and then sautéed in a hot skillet. A few simmered in barbeque sauce. It was mandatory for everyone to eat some and congratulate the cooks on their culinary skill. Then the real feast began and there was relative silence with the exception of an occasional, "Would you pass me the ...... please?" While deserts disappeared, somebody played a guitar and sang a little, someone told traditional ranch stories and yarns, some of the kids sang duets and told childish jokes, and the traditions and hospitality of the western lifestyle were on full display. Eventually, the dusk of evening settled in with an orange sun disappearing over the horizon and the good times had to come to an end. After a final swallow of Rainier beer and one final visit to the dessert table, the guests took their leave and said a few kind words to the host and hostess. When it was my turn to leave, I briefly took the host aside and said, "I, of course, don't have a cattle herd and therefore didn't have any traditional *oysters* to add to the pot. You realize that veterinarians do see other male species. We see pigs, sheep, dogs, cats, and horses. You name it we've see 'em all." There was a long pregnant silence and then a look of sudden comprehension appeared his face

He said. "You wouldn't."

I said. "I won't tell and you'll never know."

Even for you, my readers, I won't give away my secret.

GROWING OLD GRACEFULLY

Gazon was a free horse. He was a handsome gray Arabian perhaps past his prime, but in his day had been a dressage and three-day eventing horse. In spite of being a gelding he sometimes forgot himself and acted like a stallion and thus had gotten himself into serious trouble. He had become too interested in a cranky old brood mare and gotten kicked in the head. This destroyed his right eye which had to be surgically removed. His owner was a serious competitive rider and one-eyed Arab horses with a pirate eye patch don't do too well in the show ring. Thus, he had become a free horse to a good home

My wife brought him to her good home for her daughter to ride and the two were a handsome pair as they cantered over low jumps in the pasture. However, high school sports and boyfriends intervened and his career as a part-time show horse ended. So, he entered a new phase in his life as a trail horse. He had to learn how to walk, rather than prance, up a mountain trail. As he grew even older the long hours of wear and tear on his body during his earlier show years begin to catch up with him. He had developed some osteoarthritic changes in his hock. He was not lame and could move around relatively well. However, he did have difficulty lifting his right hind leg high up off the ground. Consequently, it became difficult for him to step over high logs one might encounter on a mountain trail. It is one thing to jump over rails in an arena but this is perhaps not the recommended approach with uncertain footing and solid obstacles on a mountain trail. Consequently, we sometimes had to turn around if we could not find a way to go around a log instead of over it.

On one occasion on a ride, it seemed a shame to cut the ride short because there was a moderate sized log over the trail. We got his front legs over the log but were unable to get his hind legs over. We were temporarily stymied and he stood there quietly high centered over a log unable to back up either. We jokingly said, "Where are the big carnivores when you need them?" It occurred to me that maybe we could assist him to get his hind end over. Maybe a giant cluster of helium filled balloons? He was a gentle soul and so with my wife doing rhythmic tugging on the halter to sort of get his body swaying forward and back I got behind him and put my shoulder under his rump. It seemed as if he understood what we were trying to do because when we counted one, two, three, push and my wife pulled hard on the halter and I shoved and lifted as hard as I could on his rump, he had enough impetus to clear his hind legs over the log. We had to sit down and laugh at the success of our effort. We decided that he did not appreciate our sense of humor about needing a cougar, a bear, or a great white shark. We rode on up the trail several miles, had a sandwich, an Oreo cookie snack, and gave the horses a carrot and apple core and returned by the same route. It seemed that this time he fully understood because he got his front feet over the log and stood there patiently while I got behind and boosted his rump up and over the log with my shoulder. It was much easier giving him a boost going downhill than uphill

As seasons passed, Gazon's trail rides left him pretty lame for several days afterward. We had to realize that the trail riding days were over for our 24-year-old free to a good home horse. So, we had to leave him at home in the corral. He did not do well when left behind and paced up and down the fence line whinnying in loneliness.

The Barton's were a retired couple and I occasionally saw their dog and cat. I knew that they had two old retired horses but there were never any occasions where my help was needed. The missus was a sweet delightful lady with the patience of Job. The mister was just a grumpy old man. He did, however, in his own way, appear to love his wife and faithfully cared for his animals every morning and evening. They had a big old buckskin gelding and an old Shetland pinto pony named Arnold and Danny who were inseparable best friends. Mrs. Barton was the family communicator and she called one afternoon to explain that a few days before, her husband went out in the morning to check on the horses to find that Danny the Shetland had died peacefully during the night. He couldn't get Arnold the buckskin to even walk out of his stall. They feared that if they couldn't resurrect his spirit to live, he would just starve himself to death. "Do you perhaps know of someone who has an old retired horse who might take Danny's place?" The dim little electric light bulb that usually hovered over my head suddenly lit up. I quickly called my wife and her daughter to see what they thought of the idea and whether this could be a better retirement situation for Gazon. They were more than enthusiastic. What could be better than for him than to have daily care and a constant companion in his retirement years.

The next day we loaded Gazon into the horse trailer and he whinnied sadly all the way to his potential new home. We unloaded him and introduced the two horses over the closed wooden install door. They screamed, postured and struck out at each other and we wondered if our efforts we're going to be totally in vain. Mr. Barton had a little barn with two box stalls so we decided to give him a chance to get acquainted and left Gazon there in his own stall next to Arnold the Buckskin in his stall. Mrs. Barton called daily to report and said at least they have quieted down and the barn is still standing, so maybe there was hope.

That weekend we went out to visit and test them together a second time. We were able to lead Arnold out of his stall which was unusual because he hadn't really left the barn since he had lost his friend Danny. We carefully let them approach each other until they were able to sniff noses. Finally, they settled down and we gave them a little more freedom. What transpired next was something I had never observed before. After initial screaming and striking out, old Arnold the Buckskin started licking Gazon the Arab. They started out in a nagging position where they gently chew and scratch each other's mane and withers. Then Arnold started licking and licking and licking. I don't know if a horse can smile but it seemed like Gazon stood there with an expression of friendship, camaraderie, and bliss on his dished Arabian face. Eventually they slowly walked away from the barn together and found a tasty bit of pasture grass and commenced grazing side by side, muzzle to muzzle. The introduction seemed to have gone perfectly and we went home cautiously optimistic that we had found a happy solution for the people and animals. Mrs. Barton called from time to time and said, "As far as my husband and I can, tell the two of them are never more than 10 ft apart and do everything together. They even walk together to their favorite bathroom area where they have gradually established a major manure pile."

By that time, both horses were over 25 but with the good pasture and plenty of hay in the winter they passed on into equine super senior citizenship. Three or four years later Mrs. Barton called to say that when they got up that morning, they found Arnold lying down quietly in his stall. When they checked further, they realized in fact he had laid down comfortably but permanently and quietly passed on during the night. They said that they were worried about Gazon but he was still eating and seem to be maintaining his usual habits better than expected. Only a few days later they called to say that Gazon too had been found dead that morning. They had a neighbor with a backhoe and he had dug them a large whole on the hill overlooking the house and barn. The two best friends were placed side by side in the hole and then covered over with four feet of rich topsoil.

Mrs. Barton said, "As I am sure you are well aware, my grumpy old husband Robert doesn't say too much and doesn't like to display his emotions. But I know I distinctly saw a few tears trickling down his cheeks after the whole was covered. It's not something that we would ever be able to talk about but he does look wistfully up at the hilltop from time to time when he thinks I'm not watching."

Some sad stories do have happy endings. Perhaps somewhere in Horse Heaven these two buddies are grazing side by side while the honey bees buzz around between the clover blossoms.

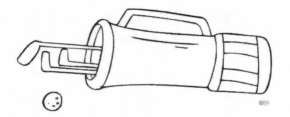

BOGEY

Sam was a retired school district administrator. He had begun 45 years earlier in the classroom as an eager middle school math and social studies teacher. Undeterred, he later moved to a similar high school position and also assumed football coaching responsibilities. Inevitably, he became athletic director, assistant principal, and then principal and finally a district superintendent in a sizable community. More recently he took a position as superintendent in a small district in a quiet community to gradually ease into retirement lifestyle. He was not a golfer but nevertheless purchased a modest home along one of the fairways of a small country golf course. In spite of occasionally finding golf balls in his yard he enjoyed the open vistas and the well-groomed countryside. He had had some early warning signs of heart issues and his doctor had recommended moderate regular exercise to keep his body and heart in shape. The golf course was perfect for this and he took daily walks along the cart paths. His walking companion was his 100lb old style black Labrador who was appropriately named Bogey. Every morning before the first golfers teed off, Sam and Bogey walked two to three miles enjoying the company of birds, rabbits, late returning raccoons and grazing deer.

Bogey was one of those dogs with retrieving so ingrained into his DNA that he always had to have something in his mouth. At

150

home he had his retrieving dummy that he carried everywhere or guarded nearby. He was also one of those dogs that would dive for rocks if you threw them into shallow water. On walks he would pick up a stick or some object to carry along. Inevitably he found golf balls which he would carry home to be added to Sam's bucket of golf balls in the garage.

Sam called early on a frosty late fall Monday morning for an appointment for Bogey. When we met in the exam room Sam quickly explained, "I think Bogey must have swallowed a golf ball. We were walking on Friday and he was carrying a golf ball in his mouth. A grouse flew up and I think in his eagerness to chase after the bird he didn't want to lose the golf ball and so he just swallowed it. He was okay until Saturday but has been eating grass and retching and trying to vomit ever since."

We did the obvious thing and took an x-ray and could see quite clearly the silhouette of a golf ball sized object in Bogey's stomach. If you looked carefully you could imagine a smiley face on it. Later that day we unzipped his belly and made a small golf ball-sized incision in his stomach and a number 3 Titleist golf ball popped out like it had been hit with a sand wedge. It rolled off the surgery drape and bounced across the surgery floor. We put a few stitches in the stomach wall, a few stitches in his belly, and sent him on his way to resume normal activity. In 10 days when we pulled the skin sutures, we had a friendly conversation with Sam about the kinds of things he should feed a dog. We said, "Golf balls are hard to digest so we would recommend not feeding too many of them."

Winter with its snow was soon upon us and Sam had to resort to quiet county roads for his morning walks. The golf course was closed for the season and was, in fact, covered with two to four feet of snow. Sam said that by the time he got his insulated boots, heavy jacket, warm gloves, scarf, and stocking cap on, he'd almost had enough exercise to meet the doctor's recommendations.

Spring finally came and the snow drifts along the tree line of the fairways melted. The golf course was pronounced open for the season and soon people were chasing little white balls up and down the long fairways and watching them disappear into little holes in the ground. Three weeks later Sam was back with Bogey. With a look of chagrin and embarrassment he said, "Well, we did it again." So: x-ray, anesthesia, surgery, sutures, dietary recommendations, and suture removal. This time it was a Top-Flite. We recommended that Sam get a muzzle for a Bogey that would prevent him from putting things in his mouth during golf course walks. Sam's wife called to say that the muzzle was working well.

However, we neglected to consider the onset of hot weather. The muzzle was fine when it was cool but it interfered with drinking and panting. One warm summer day Boogie was obviously overheating so Sam took Bogey's muzzle off. 2 days later it was Sam's wife who brought bogey in. She said, "Sam was too embarrassed to bring Bogey in himself and is feeling like a very neglectful owner. By now, anyone could anticipate and delineate the steps required to restore Bogey's digestive tract. We found a Callaway. Afterward we had a quiet conversation between Bogey and his people and were able to locate a basket muzzle which gave Bogey freedom for his mouth breathing and drinking but prevented him from putting anything larger than a peanut in his mouth. There was only one issue remaining that needed to be resolved and that was the dog's name. We all decided that from that point forward, his name would be Triple-Bogey.

EXOTIC PETS

For many centuries Russia has had a historical fur farm industry. The cold northern climate produced thick luxurious fur on mink and foxes. Fortunately, taste in clothing style and animal rights activism eventually led to drastic decline in this industry. During its heyday in the 1960's, Russian geneticists were working to improve the quality of the pelt of the Arctic fox. One of the problems was that these were still basically wild animals and understandably were difficult to work with. The producers and geneticist wondered if it was possible through selective breeding to develop a more user-friendly animal.

In the course of six generations they were able to breed arctic foxes that were small attractive friendly house pets. As these breeding programs continued there was an additional unique development. The *niceness gene* was apparently associated with the **hair coat** gene. The fur coat gradually changed and different colorations appeared such as mural, dapple, and piebald. The quality of the hair itself also changed sometimes being longer or curly or lacking the deep soft undercoat. As a result, the pelts of these animals were no longer appropriate for women's fashions and these genetic experiments we're discontinued. However, these results where noted elsewhere in the world and people wondered if it would be possible to select other species and develop designer pets.

An example is the standard dachshund which used to be a 20 to 30lb short haired dog with red, black, or black and tan coloration. They were often snappy and not recommended for families with small children. When they were bred for smaller size and wiry or long, hair coat with color patterns such as dapple, brindle, sable or piebald, they became less independent and a more loving trusting companion. The niceness gene was expressed and the resulting longhaired miniature dachshund is a sweet little dog.

Other less scrupulous pet breeders wondered if they could develop a hybrid of the ferret and the fisher. By carefully selecting offspring from the breeding program, in 6 or so generations they had also developed an animal that was much more user friendly. Ferrets weigh 2 to 4 pounds and are relatively nocturnal (crepuscular) and tend to be sleeping and quiet during the daytime. Consequently, their circadian cycle was not a good match for humans with the ferrets being disruptive and active while the humans were trying to sleep. They are, however, playful and fairly social. Fishers are larger weighing 10 to 12 pounds and are a little more active during hours of human activity. They are a relatively solitary animal. It was hoped that by developing a hybrid, they would produce a medium sized animal relatively active during daylight hours that enjoyed interacting with humans.

They had moderate success. The hybrid ate cat food and was a clean animal which was suitable for an apartment size dwelling. But this animal needed a name. It had a soft fuzzy fur coat which someone described as wooly. It was also mischievous and inquisitive (kind of a booger) and so someone jokingly suggested calling it a Wooly Booger and the name stuck. It did have an occasional aberrant behavioral characteristic that was a throwback to its predator ancestry. If the wrong button was somehow triggered it could attack something or someone rather ferociously. Luckily, it could usually distinguish between toys and the owner's fingers, but toys sometimes took a serious beating from the onslaught of these determined animals. Fortunately, their popularity never really caught on, but for a few years they did appear occasionally in pet stores.

I was acquainted with a couple and realistically, one had to say that their marriage was not made in heaven. Mary Ann was a timid caring individual and Earl was an overbearing sexist grump. He was a long-haul truck driver and was usually on the road during the week and home only on weekends. She was a homemaker and in as much as their sons had grown up, she was home alone during the week. She wasn't sure if she was happier during the week when he was gone and she was left alone, or when he was home and she had company that was typically unpleasant and grumpy. She wondered if she had a pet, that time at home would pass more quickly and the empty hours over the week would be filled. Gathering her courage, she went to the pet store, and refraining from telling the clerk about her husband Earl's disagreeable characteristics, just said, "I am looking for a pet for companionship.

The clerk thought for a moment and said, "I think I have just the one for you," and he led her over to a kennel where there was a cat sized bright-eyed beautiful brown animal.

She said, "Oh! He looks lovely."

He said, "I think you will like him but he does have some peculiar characteristics that you ought to be aware of before you purchase him. I guess the best thing to do is just demonstrate."

He said, "First of all, he's called a Wooly Booger and is a hybrid cross between two members of the weasel family, the Ferret and the Fisher. He can be playful, inquisitive, and fun to be around and he can also be warm and cuddly and really enjoys snuggling. However, when triggered he can transform into a different kind of beast." So, the clerk took the Wooly Booger out of the cage and put him on the floor where it preceded to explore and kind of lump around like a river otter. Then it came back and rolled over on its back to have its tummy rubbed.

After the ferret had been properly loved, the clerk said, "Now I will demonstrate the idiosyncrasies of his personality. Watch very carefully!" Over in the corner of the store was a pile of newspapers that were used for bedding in the animal kennels.

The clerk said, "Wooly Booger! Those newspapers." There was an amazing transformation of the little beast. It tore across the room with its claws spinning wildly for traction on the slippery floor. It ripped into the pile of newspaper and in an instant, it looked like there had been a confetti parade down the aisles of the pet store. There was shredded newspaper everywhere.

Mary Ann said, "Wow!" Then she said, "Wow!" again.

The clerk said, "I want to be very clear about this and so I will demonstrate again." In another corner of the store was a plastic waste paper basket full of empty aluminum cans that had previously contained pet foods. The clerk said, "Wooly Booger! Those food cans." And you guessed it. Again, skidding with all four wheels, the Wooly Booger dashed across the floor and attacked the waste can of empty tins. They were soon punctured with holes and there were even shards of aluminum scattered about.

Mary Ann said, "Wow!". And then she said it again. There was a brief moment of silence while she considered her options.

She said, "I understand that I need to be very careful around him but he is otherwise so soft and warm and friendly and cuddly. I just love him. I want to take him home." So along with a bag of cat food, some litter, and a bed that allowed for tunneling under the covers, Mary Ann took her brand-new pet Wooly Booger home. This was a Monday and she had a marvelous week. As she went around doing her household chores, the Wooly Booger followed behind and rubbed up against her ankles. When she took a break to watch Oprah and Dr. Phil, he jumped up on the couch with her and snuggled under her lap blanket. She had someone to talk to and could laugh at his silly antics, and he would listen to her chatter away as if he was her best friend.

On Fridays her husband was due to come home from his week on the road. It was a day of uncertainty for her because she never knew what kind of mood he would be in and she also knew that he would probably be very demanding. He typically stopped at the tavern and had a few beers before continuing on home. His time of arrival was always an uncertainty. He expected her to have a hot meal waiting for him to be served immediately after he came through the door. Fortunately, that day she got the timing right. She had a skillet of hamburger gravy over mashed potatoes with peas and carrots on the side simmering on the stove when he walked through the door.

She smiled sweetly and asked, "How was your week?" He grunted and sat down at the table and commenced eating. She felt like she had dodged a bullet and although he was his typical grumpy self, there have been no unexpected problems.

After he had finished his meal and she had served him a large slice of apple pie she said, "Earl dear! While you were gone this week, I went to the pet store and got a pet." He barely looked up for it was time for him to go into the living room and watch Wheel of Fortune. I think he enjoyed ogling Vanna. With a silent sigh of relief, Mary Ann opened the kennel door and let the Wooly Booger out to explorer and play around in the dining room and living room.

She took a big breath and ventured a second time, "While you were gone this week, I got a pet."

He looked up and said, "Pet, Schmet! Who gives a rip about your dumb little pet?"

After a while, during a commercial break, he looked up again and said, "What is that stupid looking thing?"

Mary Ann said cautiously, "It's called a Wooly Booger.

There was a poisonous silence and obviously not believing her Earl said reflexively, "Wooly Booger?   My ass!"

THE CUBAN HORSE

A post retirement Easter 2016 People to People adventure to Cuba prompted me to observe, research, and write this brief study on the Cuban horse.

In 1494 when Columbus made his second voyage to the new world, he brought pigs, cattle, and horses. (Maybe chickens and probably rats.) Horses were eventually carried from Hispaniola to Cuba where a breeding facility was established. As explorers came and went, some horses escaped or were abandoned in Mexico and the American southwest. Direct descendants of these Iberian breeds still exist in the island nation of Cuba. Today there are about 400,000 horses and additionally a total of 300,000 cattle, mules, and donkeys. The horses are grouped collectively as Criollo which strongly resemble the modern Paso Fino or Peruvian Paso breeds. Small by modern US standards, 700 – 800lb, 13 1/2 - 14 1/2 hands, tending toward darker colors, narrow but deep chested, large soft eyes, refined head, and with feet slightly larger than would be expected for a horse of that size.

In the 1950's Cuba was ruled by the corrupt dictator Fulgencio Batista who was supported by the US government. Fidel Castro, his brother Raul, and Argentinian doctor Che Guevara led what is known as the 26th of July Movement that overthrew Batista on 1 January 1959. Many wealthier Cubans felt the rebellion would fail and left Cuba thinking that their departure would be temporary. Everything they left behind was soon nationalized by the new government. In 1960, all US businesses in Cuba were nationalized and Kennedy, in tit for tat retaliation, initiated the US embargo of trade with Cuba. When no one would assist him in developing the Cuban economy, Castro turned to the USSR which was only too happy to establish a military and economic presence in the backyard of the USA. This was followed by the abortive Bay of Pigs Invasion, the Cuban missile crisis, and the collapse of the USSR in 1991.

This time is known as the "special period" in Cuba and it continues to this day. The Soviet Union had had trade agreements with Cuba whereby they supplied some of the food, machinery, and almost all of the petroleum in trade for sugar and other agriculture products. Cuba refined Russian oil in trade for part of the output. When the Soviet Union collapsed, the Russians could no longer subsidize Cuba and they pulled out. Cuba lost 80% of its imports and exports, 35% of GDP, and oil imports fell to 10% of its pre-1990 level. Cuba's industry, transportation and agriculture collapsed in the absence of industrial petroleum products. Food rationing began, power outages were common, bus waits could be 3 hours, and the average Cuban lost 20lb of body weight.

Showing amazing resilience, the Cubans survived, albeit somewhat marginally. Australian aid and technology arrived especially in agriculture with raised garden beds, rooftop gardens, and community gardens wherever there was vacant urban space. Transportation was improvised with semi-trucks converted to 300 passenger people haulers, box trucks converted to buses, importation of 1.5 million Chinese bicycles which fell apart, and resurrection of late 1950's Chevrolet cars (still seen in large numbers on urban Cuban streets). Almost everything was, and is, owned by the state including the vintage cars. Food is subsidized but you must have a ration card, everyone is guaranteed a government job if they want it, and free education and medicine is available for everyone. Everyone travels with a shopping bag in hope that they might pass a government store and discover that a scarce item was in stock. Such items could sell out in minutes. There is one MD for every 25 families. However, wages in government jobs are $20 - $40 per month but it takes $360 for a family of four to subsist. Consequently, both parents work as perhaps do older children and outside private sources of income must be arranged. Everybody hustles. Anything the people can produce locally from handicrafts to home grown food is available almost everywhere. Trash has value and none is left in the streets. The absence of fast food also keeps the streets clean as do countless ownerless street dogs. Last year (2015) Cuba had 1 million tourists from mainly Europe and Canada providing desperately needed foreign exchange to purchase technology, oil, and machinery. Cuba trades doctors and medical technology to Venezuela for oil.

All this has led to the resurrection of the utilitarian horse in Cuba. Horses seem to be ubiquitous with about one horse for every 25 people and all of them serving a useful purpose. (In contrast in the US there is about one horse for every 110 people with a much lower utilization efficiency). Cuban horses are staked out everywhere there is grass, often only by a halter rope and still saddled or harnessed. Fences, trees, bushes, rocks, and old tires all serve as hitching posts. Most horses are used to pull light carts or wagons in a single hitch at a trot while a few are under saddle moving at a running walk like a Paso Fino. They compete, at 6 mph wearing blinkers, with bus traffic going 60 mph on provincial highways and must obey all traffic laws. Looking down a quiet city street you might see 8 or 10 carts hauling people or goods with horses in fact outnumbered automobiles. They cost $250 to $300. Surely there must be animal/auto collisions but I saw the carriages causing no apparent traffic problems. Perhaps this is due to the fact that horses are a way of life in Cuba and automobile drivers are more educated and considerate. Our bus made frequent hard stops to avoid a lone small horse pulling a two or four wheeled cart down a highway.

Many of the cart horses were stallions but this wasn't for financial reasons since veterinary services were free including vaccinations and deworming. Urban cart horses had poop catchers suspended from the shafts and there was no manure in the streets. Country roads were a little more fertilized. All horses were shod with most having tow clips on the shoes. Occasionally you could hear a shoe jingle indicating it was loose and the need to be reset but feet seemed well cared for considering they were traveling mostly on paved surfaces. They seemed amazingly universally docile and willingly shifting from a walk to a trot with a vocal click.

Operating a city carriage required a license and necessitated 4 horses: one for the morning, one for the afternoon, and two resting at home. At the end of the day the operator drove one horse home leading the other. Little hay was available and apparently no grain with the horses managing on pasture alone. Most were lean but not poor.

My fellow travelers pointed out poor horses to me wanting a comment from a veterinarian but I felt most were thin because they were aged. Horse meat is eaten since there is a general shortage of protein. It is illegal to eat a cow without government permission with a significant fine. The horses were not heavy enough for farm labor and oxen teams were frequently seen plowing small fields due to the tractor shortage.

Carts came in all forms from two wheeled to four wheeled, tires of steel, hard rubber, bicycle rubber or even automotive, sprung or unsprung, fancy or plain, covered or open, and carrying from two to the legal maximum of eight passengers. There is no exchange money to buy carts on the world market so they must construct and improvise locally with no two carts being the same. Some even had an automotive battery to power a boom box and many allowed bicyclists to be towed behind

Temperature was in the low to mid 90's and it was an issue for the horses. Their thin skin and short hair coat seemed to help and none seemed to sweat profusely. However, when at rest they breathed heavily to assist in cooling.

Cuba is a strange juxtaposition of good education, modern medicine, and technology awaiting financing and development against a barter/trade/ subsistence existence. The people seem resolute, frustrated, and eagerly await the better times they see in the future.

VETERINARY OPHTHAMOLOGY

Dr. Frank was beyond retirement age but he loved teaching and was too valuable a faculty resource to be put out to pasture. He began his career as a private practitioner and then returned to school to get his Ph.D. and eventually join the veterinary school faculty. With regard to large animal veterinary medicine, he had pretty much ***been there and done that***. He taught the clinical sections, where students actually examine and treat live animals. He could be a little grumpy and was definitely a no-nonsense kind of person but his vast knowledge and experience were appreciated by all his future veterinarians.

We were eager to learn, bright-eyed, and bushy-tailed. We were finally at the stage of our education where we could start

practicing what we had learned and spent
in either small animal or large animal clini
occasionally lulls in the clinical schedule
treated and there was nothing further ne
Sometimes he would gather the students on
feed room and we would sit on the bales of ha
us with stories of the *good old days*. When he
of timothy hay out of a bale to chew on, we kne ... were about
to be regaled to one of his legendary stories. One point he liked to
make was that while there certainly was unlimited knowledge to
be gained from our books and lectures, the experience of older
veterinarians could also be invaluable as we developed our skills.

Dr. Frank said, "After I graduated from school, I worked for
an old veterinarian who must have been about as old as I am now.
Doc, as we called him, was a great mentor and just as we're doing
now, Doc and I sometimes sat around and talked about cases he
dealt with during his long career. On one occasion this
information served me especially well."

Dr. Frank continued, "A rancher called me out one day to look
at one of his Hereford bulls. He told me that the animal seemed to
be a little off his feed, and was unsteady on his feet. It was early
spring and it was time to turn the bull out to visit with the cows
but he was concerned that the bull wouldn't be up to the task."

Dr. Frank smiled and added, "You may not believe this but we
were out of the horse and buggy era by then but I didn't have a
big fancy pickup truck with a veterinary box on the back. I drove
an old Chevy coupe in those days and if you pulled the back seat
out, you had this large space behind the driver's seat extending
clear back into the trunk. We jokingly said that my coupe could
double as a hearse in a pinch. I called her Betty after my first
girlfriend; who dumped me by the way. I drove Betty the Chevy
out to the ranch and with the rancher on his horse and his dog

we worked the unsteady bull up into the cattle chute. ...ed like he had lost some weight but his vitals were still ...thin normal range. I stood back to look him over and finally realized that there was something peculiar about his head. He seemed to have some sort of a minor tremor and when I looked more closely, I discovered that he was cross-eyed. I pointed this out to the rancher and he said, 'This is only his second breedin' season and he certainly wuz fine last year and on through the winter.' I had to admit to the rancher that I had never seen anything quite like this before and was uncertain as to what the cause might be."

Dr. Frank paused to collect his thoughts and then went on, "I'm sure you have all had moments when you were trying to remember something; a word, a date, or whatever and finally had to give up. And then from out of nowhere, the thing you were trying to remember suddenly pops into your head. I must have had just such a moment. I told the rancher that just this past winter Doc and I had been talking and he was telling me about some of the strange cases he had seen in his career and, I just now realized that this was just like one of them. Doc told me how he had treated it and didn't know what caused it and didn't know why the treatment worked but you can't argue with success."

Then Dr. Frank told us how he had treated the cross-eyed bull saying, "I got my bovine stomach tube which was actually just 10-foot length of three-quarter inch automotive radiator hose. To use it in the normal fashion you put a gag in a cow's mouth which allows you to pass the hose down the esophagus into the cow's stomach but it prevents the cow from being able to chew on the hose. But we were going to use it on the other end of the digestive system."

He continued, "I again told the rancher that I didn't know how or why the treatment works but I was pretty sure it would be the appropriate thing to do."

I told the rancher, "Go to the front of the cattle chute and watch the bull's eyes. I'm going to feed this hose up into the bull's rectum and make an airtight seal by putting a purse string suture around it. Then I'm going to blow into the hose and if we increase the pressure enough and everything works as expected we should be able to cure your bull. So, you watch his eyes and when they are pointed straight ahead you signal to me."

"You can imagine the look of serious doubt that appeared on the rancher's face, said Dr. Frank. "Nevertheless, I huffed and puffed and blew as hard as I could into the end of the hose. I almost had to stop and burst out laughing when I saw the look of total disbelief appear on the rancher's face. Finally, he signaled like a flagman trying to stop a freight train. I put my thumb over the end of the hose and held it there for about 5 minutes while we talked about the weather and the price of the cattle at the sales yard. Finally, with considerable apprehension, I very carefully pulled the hose out. We waited and watched and unbelievably, although the eyes were still twitching a little bit, something we call nystagmus, they straightened out and appeared totally normal. After waiting a while to make sure things were stabilized, we turned the bull out and he looked around, snorted, and commenced bellowing which was his way of signaling to the cows and he was ready and willing."

Dr. Frank grinned and said "We stood around and laughed and talked and marveled about it. Eventually, I got back in Betty the Chevy and went on with the rest of my ranch calls."

Dr. Frank told us that a few weeks later he was doing some health checks at the sales barn and happened to meet the rancher in the bleachers. I asked him, "How did things turn out with your bull?

The rancher said, "Jus' fine but a peculiar thang happened that you might find dang curious. I was out checking my girls t'other day and I seen thet my neighbor was also out in his back 40 ridin' his herd too. We moseyed over t'the fence, rolled a smoke, and chewed the fat for a while about the usual. You know, the weather, the price of cattle.

My neighbor said, 'I 'served a funny thang this morning. I ain't quite sure what to make of it. You see my two bulls over yonder? They're both plumb cross eyed and staggerin' around like two drunks thet spent too much time hangin' out at the tavern last night.'

I told my neighbor, 'What a strange coincident. A few weeks back, I brung Dr. Frank out to eyeball my bull who had the same ailment. I marveled if there ain't something catchin' going 'round. But you know, Dr Frank fixed my bull right up and as you can spy him over there messin' with the cows, he's doin' just fine. It didn't seem too tuff 'n I bet you that between you'n me we outta be able to make your bulls right too. So, we drove one of my neighbor's bulls inta the chute and squoze him up. I 'splained what I aimed to do. We grubbed up an ol' piece of garden hose and whittled on one end with a case knife to make it round and smooth like a baby's butt. Since I knowed what I wuz doin', I figured I'd do the blowin' and have my neighbor do the watchin'. So, we shoved thet garden hose right up the bull's rear end but didn't have any way to put a string on it, so I just squeezed his butt right tight with my left hand. My neighbor hung out by the bull's head to watch them eyeballs and to holler if there was anything goin' on. I huffed and puffed and huffed and puffed but just couldn't seem to get 'er done. My neighbor said he could spy

168

the eyeballs twitchin' but then they slithered right back. I ran out of air and had to quit or I was gonna pass out"

My neighbor said, 'I bet I got more wind than y'all an' maybe I can blow hard 'nough to get 'er done.' So, we figgered to swap places and give 'er 'nother go. The neighbor hauled the hose plumb out and turned it around and shoved the other end back in.

I asked him, 'Why in hell d'you do thet?'

He said, 'Well stupid. I didn't want to put my mouth on the same end you'd been blowin' on.'"

GIRLFRIEND

After 38 years in a career I loved, it was time to hang it up. I had literally been limping along on anti-inflammatories for the last few years. I must have had a cast iron gut because I was taking the equivalent of twelve 200 mg ibuprofen capsules every day. I had X-rayed my own hips and shown them to an orthopedic surgeon in a nearby town. He commented, "Where did you get these X-rays? They show what I need to see but the view is a little bit unusual."

I smiled and said, "They were taken by a veterinarian with whom I'm well acquainted." He looked at me quizzically for a moment and then he too smiled. We examined the X-rays and he said, "As I'm sure you are well aware, both your hips should be replaced. We usually wait about 6 months between the surgeries.

I said, "Do you ever do both of them at the same time?

He replied, "I never have but I guess there is no reason not to."

I said, "Well, if you are willing, I will be your first bilateral hip replacement Guinea Pig"

But before I underwent the knife, I had one more task to complete. We had a client in a nearby town who rescued Border Collies. Some Border Collies are so neurotic that they don't make suitable pets. Realizing this, Mike and his wife had fenced-in a 1-acre exercise area for these dogs. He brought all the dogs that he took in to us for checkups, vaccinations, and neutering. In recognition for his huge effort in rescuing these dogs, we provided these services at cost. If and when he found forever homes, part of the rehoming fees reimbursed him for the fees we had charged him and any other costs.

So that was how I met Piper. Mike had brought her to us for vaccinations and to be spayed. She was about a year old and was a beautiful black and white border collie cross from southern Idaho. She loved people, especially if they had an unlimited supply of tummy rubs and ear scratches. We gave her a quick grooming and a large dose of love before we anesthetized her and put her on the table. It didn't take long to surgically remove her baby factory. I sat with her for a few minutes as she was recovering from the anesthetic. She crawled slowly over to be next to me and put her head in my lap. I felt something tug at my heartstrings. When I visited her the next morning, she obviously recognized me and licked my hand when I massaged the top of her head and ears. Then I drove to a nearby town for installation of my two new store-bought hips

Now, fast forward a month post-surgery for Piper and me. I had thrown away my walker in disgust and was gimping around pretty well but being recently single and no longer having a job to fill my days, I discovered that my house was pretty big and empty. During a moment of self-pity, I got on the phone and called Mike. I said, "Mike, this is Dr Fred. Do you still have that dog Piper that I spayed about a month ago?"

There was a momentary silence and I dreaded what the answer might be. After all, how could anybody not want such a wonderful dog. Then Mike said, "I'll have her there in half an hour."

Do you remember your teenage years? You had become unaccountably infatuated with someone and when walking down the hall between classes look up and suddenly, they were there. Your heart races and your face gets flushed. Well that's the way I felt when I realized I would soon have a new girlfriend.

When Mike delivered her to my house, I greeted them on my front porch. It was a warm Indian summer day and I sat down on the steps. Piper seemed to remember me and trotted right up and put her head in my lap. We have rarely been separated ever since.

You can only guess what the other part of her ancestry is. We've never done a DNA test. She has the soft wooly undercoat and a tail that curls up over her back that is typical of some of the northern breeds. In the winter she likes to lie on my freezing cold front porch and just watch and listen. Cold doesn't seem to bother her. I jokingly say that since she is a northern herding dog, someday we plan to go to the arctic to herd musk ox. Little by little she has trained me to understand her language. She can bark for: Outside, Food, Squirrels, Birds, Hurry up! Let's go! and Why aren't you sharing that food with me? She probably does a better job of understanding me than I do her. She understands Inside, Outside, Food, Load up, Where's the mouse? Where's the kitty? and Feed the horses. When her feet are muddy, she understands Give me a foot, Now the other foot, and Turn around (so I can wipe down the back feet). At home she sleeps pretty much wherever she wants but it is always where she can watch me. When we are away from home, she chooses to lie down next to my feet usually making physical contact. That way she knows that if I get up and move, she will be alerted. She likes Oreo Cookies too.

The horses seem to travel better on mountain trails if she is out in front. They know that she has cleared the trail of any dangerous sasquatches, vultures, salt water crocodiles, giant vampire bats, and rabid squirrels or chipmunks. Her favorite place to be is probably in my pop-up camper. Floor space is severely limited and to avoid trampling her, I let her stay on the bed over the truck cab. I know she smiles when she looks down to see what I am doing. She can look out the screened windows from the bed and watch for deer, elk, grouse, and small woodland rodents. When I am reincarnated in my next life as a twenty something young man looking for a date, I want Piper with me because she is an absolute magnet for the ladies. I won't need to struggle for an awkward opening line. I'll just let her make the introductions for me and the ice will be broken.

A ROOM WITH A VIEW

The USFS used to provide good summer jobs for young people just out of high school or attending college. Times have changed and now trail maintenance and construction and firefighting positions are largely contracted out. When I graduated from high school and during the summers of my university years, I was the foreman of the trail crew responsible for maintaining trails on Forest Service land in Kittitas County. Later, when I was attending veterinary school, I had the position of Wilderness Ranger and I spent my summers working from a camp 10 miles up a trail deep into Wenatchee National Forest at Waptus Lake.

Usually, the job started early in June but one year there had been especially deep snow through the winter and a cool spring so the backcountry was still inaccessible due to deep lingering snowpack. Something had to be done to keep me occupied until I could lead my pack string into the mountains so it was decided to put me in the construction business. It was a non-union job prefabricating mountain thrones otherwise known as Wallowa toilets. They were essentially two boxes. One was a flat box about two and a half feet wide, 5 feet long, and about 6 inches deep. This made the base of the mountain throne. The other was a box that was about two and a half feet on each side. It conveniently had a hole in it shaped like a toilet seat and a hinged lid that could drop down over to cover the hole. It did not have walls, a flush handle, a hand washing basin, a toilet paper holder, or even a mirror. Since there was no door, it didn't have a crescent shaped moon cutout either.

Using redwood, because of its light weight and rot resistance qualities, I manufacturing the parts for 40 toilets. Because it was going to be a public toilet, I secretly initialed the inside of the lid on each one. They were appropriate for use under the rustic conditions of the backcountry and could be broken down, mantied up (wrapped up in heavy canvas) and carried two to a mule into the backcountry

Once the snow melted and the trails opened up it was my job to pack these toilets into the backcountry and find appropriate places to plant them near popular campsites. Occasionally, I encountered backpackers who asked. "What are those packages that your mules are carrying?"

I replied, "They are powder rooms for the lady hikers."

Planting involved finding a suitable private location and digging a hole. It was not always an easy task. You attempted to find a place camouflaged by brush or trees but digging in those areas was usually complicated by the extensive root systems. Next you unpacked the parts and nailed them together and installed them over the newly dug hole. Then you had to build a trail to this secluded location and put up a sign pointing in the proper direction. Being too lazy to construct two duplicate installations I made the executive decision to designate each one a unisex facility compatible for both sexes. These were the easy ones.

Other locations could be much more complicated. The big issue was finding enough dirt to dig a hole that was deep enough. I was 16 miles in, near a place called Dutch Miller Gap. It's a fascinating geological location because there is a small pond in the saddle between two river valleys. During the spring runoff, some of the water goes west towards Puget Sound and some of the water goes east down the Yakima River to the Columbia eventually meeting the Pacific saltwater by a more circuitous route.

I dug at least 6 test holes but couldn't find more than one foot of dirt. The holes were supposed to be at least 3 feet deep. Finally, I managed to dig a two-foot hole and by doing careful mortarless masonry, stacked up enough flat rocks around it to make a 3 ½ foot deep hole. With great satisfaction and pride of accomplishment I installed the toilet over the hole and paused for an Oreo Cookie snack and a drink from the ice-cold stream.

The site was hidden from the camp area and the trail but was literally located on a cliff safely and sanitarily distant from a 300-foot water cascade. You could sit there in total solitude reading your Sears catalog or Reader's Digest and look out over the hazy valley 3000 feet below. You could see the Waptus River and Lake. You could see the snowcapped Stuart Range. You could see the green fields of the very distant Kittitas Valley. You could see hawks riding the thermals.

What a great place to go!

SPECIAL

Ribbons had been a truly special equine member of the family. Initially she belonged to a young lady who, after a night of partying, managed to destroy a telephone pole with her car. The stupid pole just jumped out in front of her and she didn't have time to avoid it. The magistrate had declared that along with her driving citation, she would be allowed to pay for the cost of pole replacement as well. This was how the $400 purchase price for Ribbons was determined and how her ownership was transferred from the young lady to a horse loving young family. She was a bright cherry red bay quarter horse mare who was willing and able to do just about anything you asked of her.

She happily carried a mother and her two daughters, one in front and one behind, as they ventured into the local neighborhood woods and trails. She once entered and explored

177

the house basement and then negotiated the carpeted curving stairway up to the main floor of their split-level house. On a hot summer day, on a dare, she carried her bareback mistress out onto a dock and without hesitation jumped off the end into Puget Sound. She was the queen of a barnyard menagerie that included a milk cow, a pig, an obnoxious butting goat, a frightening honking wing flapping butt pinching white goose, and a flock of red leghorn laying hens.

A divorce necessitated that the mother complete a university degree to support her family. So, Mom, two daughters, two horses (Ribbons and Gazon), a Brittany Spaniel (Benjamin Big Boy Feather Finder), and three cats (White Lightning, Liebchen, and Angie), relocated to Ellensburg to attend Central Washington University.

I was introduced to this family when White Lightning was collected by an animal control officer in the pet forbidden vicinity of University student family housing. She promptly delivered five kittens soon after at the local animal shelter. Getting her out of jail meant paying her impound fee and providing documentation that she had been spayed. I was no match for the sad eyes of a mother and her two daughters when they explained their plight and their lack of funds to meet the legal requirements of the situation.

Ultimately, White Lightning received a complimentary surgical procedure and I was adopted into the family to also begin a relationship with Ribbons, the very special horse. We didn't have enough horses for the enlarged family so sometimes we did trail rides with Ribbons carrying double and the other two people alternating between Gazon the Arabian and a mountain bike named Schwinn.

We once did a two-night weekend horse camping trip to a secret meadow I knew from my Forest Service days. I was assured that Ribbons loved hanging around the camp and would not wander off or try and escape. One morning however, while wearing hobbles and dragging a halter rope, she led her trail mate away from camp galloping deeper into the mountains. Fearing for their safety (and our loss of transportation), we ran uphill after them until we finally collapsed exhausted and overheated on a rock. Knowing that we had been outsmarted, we contemplated how we were going to find them. Resigning ourselves to continuing our horseless hike we continued on up the trail. Just around the next bend we encountered our wayward horses. The footprints in the trail indicated that they had turned around and where coming back down off the mountain. The green stains on their lips and the grass stems protruding from the corners of their mouths indicated that they had also been collecting some additional breakfast items. We wondered if, in fact, Ribbons had enjoyed her early morning excursion and was coming back to camp hoping to share in our huckleberry pancake and syrup breakfast.

With Benjamin the dog out front scouting the trail ahead and determining that the way it was safe, no hill was too steep or mud hole too deep for Ribbons not to carry us safely on. Weekend by weekend I was able to guide my new family and reexplore all the trails and routes through the country I knew from my previous Forest Service summer jobs.

I had veterinary office hours until noon on Saturdays. As soon as I could lock the doors, I would rush home where my wife had lunches prepared and Ribbons and her pasture mates already loaded into the trailer. Time was limited so we rode as hard and fast as the terrain and the horse's conditioning allowed. Chipmunks, squirrels, and other small rodents scampered out of the way as we came thundering past. With Ribbons leading the way and loving what she was doing, we automatically accelerated into a trot when the footing of the trail allowed.

Ribbons competed in western horseback games (gymkhanas), assisted with trick or treating by wearing a giant four-legged ghost costume, wore sleigh bells for Christmas caroling, and carried countless special needs children from my wife's special education classroom when they had picnic days. She could do it all

The years flew by and we added countless new trails to our riding inventory. With Ribbons progressing into equine senior citizenship, we rode one weekend into the White River country above Lake Wenatchee. We camped overnight in a high mountain glacial cirque with marmots making piercing alarm whistles from their rocky lookouts. When the sun rose through the morning mist it was time to pack up and return home. After putting out the fire and breaking camp, we began our ride back down to the trailhead. The heavy dew on the trailside ferns drenched our boots and pantlegs. Later we dismounted to lead the horses across a short broken-backed log bridge over a quiet stream. I watched in horror as Ribbons stepped off the edge of the bridge and fell four feet to land heavily on her side on a sandy gravelly spot in the stream bed below. We held our breath anxiously until she quickly scrambled back up onto her feet. We cut some brush to make a path and get her up out of the stream bed until she eventually stood shakily back on the trail. We checked her over to find that amazingly, she only had some minor cuts and scrapes. I was standing by her head to rub her muzzle and give her some reassurance when the slanting early morning sunlight shown into her eyes. To my dismay, I saw the telltale signs of periodic ophthalmia: light sensitivity, inflammation and a cloudy anterior chamber and cornea. Its cause is poorly understood but it is the most common cause of blindness in horses.

This was to be Ribbons last mountain pack trip or ride. The early morning dimness of the heavy old growth forest did not provide enough light for Ribbons to find her way so using her pasture buddy as a seeing eye horse, we slowly led her down out of the mountains.

Periodic ophthalmia, or moon blindness, has reoccurring episodes of inflammation, each of which further reduces vision. Gazon the Arabian, who ironically only had one eye, became her constant pasture companion and they grazed side by side on through the summer. He seemed to realize that Ribbons needed his assistance to negotiate her more restricted world. If he strayed too far, they would nicker to each other until she could relocate him and continue grazing. With fall came shorter days and more hours of darkness and life became increasing difficult for Ribbons. She could find her way into the stall to eat hay but sadly became more fearful in her restricted enclosed environment. Sudden noises could startle her and her instinct told her to escape the confines of the barn out to the relative safety of the pasture. If she turned the right way, she could find the door from the stall. If she turned the wrong way, she smacked her head painfully into the stall wall. Each successive day became more of a trial and her usual self-confidence was reduced to an existence of fear. Some horses can calmly manage the transition into total blindness but this was not the case with Ribbons.

We had reached the point where there was no alternative to putting her down. The horses had a favorite corner of the pasture where they liked to stand. I borrowed the neighbor's backhoe and dug a large deep hole nearby. With the cats watching from the barn door and Ribbon's old canine trail companion Benjamin Big Boy Feather Finder attending nearby, we all said our tearful good-byes. I was abandoned buy the rest of my family when the time came to give her the lethal injection. With a deep sigh she collapsed heavily to the ground next to the hole. My stethoscope confirmed that her heart had stopped and I eased her into the hole and backfilled with the backhoe. A large rock, excavated by the backhoe when digging the hole, was placed on top of the dirt mound to mark her final resting place.

Through the years she has been replaced by other fine horses but her image still comes to mind when I get out the saddle and headstall that she had once worn.

COINCIDENCE

Coincidence: "A remarkable occurrence of events or circumstances without apparent causal connection"

My veterinary practice partner in Mission, B C Canada was of German descent and still had family living in Berlin. German names sometimes include several middle names honoring grandparents. Consequently, Dr. Mark Jürgen Max Edwin Schmidt went by the name Paddy. Every winter he took a 6-week vacation to visit and ski with his family at Zermatt and Chamonix in Switzerland. Needless to say, the impact on me was significant because I had to run the practice short-handed in his absence. Our associate was enthusiastic, but was a recent vet school graduate and needed a significant level of assistance even to perform fairly routine tasks. Anticipating a certain level of burnout, my family

183

and I had planned a bareboat sailing vacation in the British Virgin Islands of the Caribbean upon my partner's return.

It was a Friday afternoon in late February and Paddy had just returned from Europe the night before. Our plan was to take the red-eye flight out of Seattle on Saturday evening. There was one last routine surgery to complete: spaying a brown cuddly fuzzy puppy that was a cross between a miniature poodle and a mystery pooch. This was before the era of designer puppies but she would definitely have fit into that category. My assistant Nancy quietly held her while I eased a tiny needle into the vein in her foreleg to inject the anesthetic. She wagged her tail twice and licked my offending hand before she slumped quietly down on the preparation table. It didn't take long to shave her tummy and remove the unnecessary reproductive parts. I finished by putting 10 neat little stitches in her tummy and we moved her into the recovery kennel where we placed her under a prewarmed blanket. It was late in the day so we elected to observe her overnight to be picked up by her family in the morning. I checked on her one last time before turning the lights out and stepping outside into the rain of March. I drove home carefully in the dark and slanting downpour.

Perhaps anticipating my state of mind and physical fatigue, my wife greeted me at the door with a long warm hug and a kiss. She said, "I've got some hot potato soup and a toasted cheese sandwich on the stove. I've already packed your passport, swim trunks, mask, snorkel, fins, and sun screen. I don't think we will need anything else. We can leave first thing in the morning."

It was a long inconvenient fight through Houston, Miami, and finally arriving in San Juan Puerto Rico where we had to spend the night in a questionable hotel. In the morning we boarded a twin-engine propeller aircraft for the bouncy fight south to the Leeward Islands of the Lesser Antilles. The flight attendant had to ask several of the passengers to relocate when a very oversized gentleman boarded and had been assigned a seat in the rear of the airplane. The aircraft couldn't fly with such an unbalanced load. It was too noisy to sleep or to maintain a conversation so we tried to read and sip on our plastic glass of Diet Coke without spilling and ration the snack which contained at least 12 peanuts.

Finally, we bounced to a landing and rolled to a stop on Beef Island, the location of the airport on Tortola in the British Virgin Islands. Only about 12 passengers got off and we collected our luggage from the pile where they had been dumped on the tarmac. The breeze off the bay was refreshing after the stuffy ride in the airplane. We could see the fronds of the palm trees fluttering off in the distance silhouetted by the setting sun. Banded doves cooed romantically from nearby trees. Our vacation and respite from the cold and wet of coastal British Columbia was finally about to begin.

We queued up (that's what you do in British speaking parts of the world) with passports in hand to go through customs. The agents appeared to be finishing up their tea and were in no hurry to facilitate our entry into their country. We waited patiently not wanting to bring undue attention to ourselves. Without intending to and without realizing it, I found myself eavesdropping on the conversation of a mother and young daughter just in front of us in the line.

The daughter said, "I'm really worried about Fluffy. Are you sure that Dad will remember to pick her up?"

The mother replied smiling, "Dad loves her too and I'm sure he will remember. I know she will be just fine after her surgery."

Fussing with the scrunchie in her hair the daughter asked, "Do you know what they did to her?"

Mom replied, "I'm not sure but I expect the doctor will be glad to answer your questions when we take her in to get her stitches removed."

I tried not to be nosy but my curiosity got the better of me. I ventured, "It sounds like you took a pet to the veterinarian."

Mom replied, "Yes, we took our dog Fluffy in to be spayed just two days ago and as you can see my daughter Jenny is a little worried about her."

I smiled and said, " I just happen to be a veterinarian. This is a very routine procedure for a doctor and it can be easy for us to forget how concerned pet owners can be. There are perhaps thousands of dogs spayed every day and I can assure you they will all be just fine." I could sense that Jenny had questions on her mind but was too shy to ask them.

Mom asked "Where is your practice?"

I replied, "Canada."

Mom said, "Oh! You don't really sound like a Canadian.

I responded, "Well actually, I'm from the US but we emigrated to Canada about 5 years ago. I'm still learning to speak Canadian."

Jenny asked shyly, "Where do you live in Canada?"

I said, "In British Columbia."

Jenny said, "Oh that's where we live too. We live in Mission."

Mom gave her daughter I look as if to say, "I don't think you should be telling a stranger quite so much about yourself."

Sensing this, I wasn't sure if it was appropriate to continue the conversation but I couldn't help myself. I asked, "What does your dog look like?"

Jenny, temporarily forgetting her shyness, said, "Her name is Fluffy. She's brown and cuddly and fuzzy and I love her so much. We think she's part poodle and part something else. Dad teases me and says she is just some sort of a mongrel but I think she's really special."

At this point I couldn't contain myself and I said, "Isn't that an amazing coincidence? You are Jenny and Sarah Brown and you live on Cedar Valley Road.

Their eyes widened in astonishment. "How do you know that?" Sarah Brown asked.

I was a little amazed myself and said, "Well, I live on Best Road just off of Cedar Valley Road. We are almost neighbors. And I am Dr. Fred and I spayed Fluffy two days ago just before we left Mission for this vacation."

Just then the customs agents had finally finished their tea and were strolling over to check us in. It turns out the Browns were on a sailing vacation also and were meeting a relative. We shared a taxi into Road Town where we eventually checked in and boarded our sailboat which was to be our floating hotel for the next week. In the overall scheme of the universe anything can happen, but it still seems incredible to meet neighbors 2800 miles from home, let alone be their family veterinarian. We encountered them again one evening while anchored near the iconic place *The Baths* on the island of Virgin Gorda,.and shared an evening *Sundowner* drink while watching the tropical sun go down.

Two weeks later we had a mini re-union when the Browns brought Fluffy in to have her stitches removed. She wagged her tail and licked my hand. Sarah and Jenny each got a hug because, after all, we were now good friends.

THE END

THE WHOLE FAMN DAMILY

Made in the USA
Monee, IL
18 February 2020

21936689R00111